Tears and Tales

Russell A. Vassallo

Cover Design: Mila Ryk
Edited By: Susan Stafford

ISBN# 0-9740841-6-6

Tears and Tales
Russell A. Vassallo

ISBN# 0-9740841-6-6
Retail Price $ 18.95 US
Printed in the USA, Canada and Europe

Whitehall Publishing
PO Box 548
Yellville, Arkansas USA 72687
info@whitehallpublishing.com

To learn more about Russell A. Vassallo or to order additional books via the web, visit him at **www.krazyduck.com.** You can also order books at TheCompletePet.com, via Amazon.com, by calling 800-700-5096 or via mail order through Whitehall Publishing at the above address.

To contact our author, e-mail Russ@krazyduck.com

Table of Contents

Tears and Tales

Dedication

To my wife Virginia who encouraged me to write just for the sake of writing. Without her inspiration all the animals that have been part of my life would have passed unnoted.

Acknowledgment

I gratefully acknowledge the countless hours contributed by my wife, Virginia, who encouraged me, edited my work, fought me when I became discouraged and proffered just the right mix of criticism and praise.

To Joan Sparks who read each new story and became my fan.

I further acknowledge Bonnie Marlewski-Probert who published my very first story, educated me in the practicalities of publishing and stood by my side as publication unfolded. To Stephen King, who taught me that the adverb is not my friend.

To Laine Raia for her brilliant editorial work and encouragement. She is the Good Samaritan who stopped to help a stranger. Nor can I forget my professional editor, Susan Stafford, the editor with a heart.

And finally, to my friend and veterinarian, Chuck Keiser, who cried along with me when I lost an animal friend. To those whose names I may never know, to those who joined in encouraging me, I thank you all for making this possible.

Biography
Russell A. Vassallo

Russell A Vassallo was born in Newark, NJ on April 24, 1934. Besieged by asthma, bronchial pneumonia and mastoiditis he spent his winters alone and bedridden where his favorite pastime was reading the classics.

Russ attended Seton Hall University where he majored in Political Science and Literature. His penchant for words helped to earn him part of his college tuition by writing short stories for other students. He entered Seton Hall University School of Law in September 1958 and graduated three years later. Due to financial circumstances at home, he did not apply for admission to the NJ Bar for ten years. In the interim, he worked for two major insurance companies as an investigator and started his own investigation and subpoena business. Ten years later, Russ passed the NJ Bar exam on the first try and became a successful attorney.

While practicing law he married and raised four children. His first marriage ended and in 1983 he met his present wife, Virginia, who encouraged him to battle back against depression by writing short stories. To his surprise, he discovered that growing older and maturing had given him more insight and depth for his writing.

Russ and Virginia now live on their farm in rural Kentucky with six horses, two dogs and five cats all of whom provide Russ with countless stories for upcoming volumes of Tears and Tales!

Introduction

I was an only child for seven years, my only sibling being a Pomeranian named Palsy. But Palsy was a test of will of a difficult marriage between mom and dad. My father argued I should not be alone. Mother argued having an animal was not acceptable. At the start, Dad prevailed and Palsy came into my life, but only until Mother found a legitimate excuse to pass him off to a neighbor. And thus, I lost my friend and mourned him as I have mourned the passing of other animal friends.

I always thought I'd write "the" great American novel, romance, action, history. But, alas, my friends have all been animals or most of them, anyway --and thus those stories which occurred to me most readily were the stories of my friends, their rescues, lives, friendships and deaths. The words and sentiments seemed to flow naturally, perhaps because they were sincerely felt. As friends and associates read my stories they, too, were touched by the sentiments therein.

Each of the stories you will read in Tears and Tails is based on actual animals I have been fortunate enough to befriend in my life. In some cases, I had to use supposition and creative ability to fill out the story since I did not always know the early history of each animal. Essentially, though, the information is true and I still find myself rather tearful when I read and edit the stories.

There is no better way to immortalize a friend than to write about him and have the work published. In that way, he assumes a character and life almost eternal; for as long as there are readers, my animals live. That is my hope, my dream, that all the animal friends who have touched me in various ways will never die. In the telling of their stories, future generations will come to know them too.

There are animals that come into our lives in passive ways, achieving no monumental quality other than being there. And others that spark our existence, work magical deeds and bring us to life. There roles are not always defined in my stories because it was not my intent to focus on myself, but rather on the animals. Sweet Pea, for example, inspired the story *Git*, because she arrived when Tribute was dying of cancer. At first I resented her. I felt she came prematurely to replace my beloved friend. I pitied her. I fed her. I took her in, but I vastly resented her. And the story of that resentment would make a tale in and of itself, but again, I was focusing on Sweet Pea and not myself.

Spunky, the half Shar Pei/Pit Bull mix, who inspired *God of All Creatures,* was shackled to a dog house on an eighteen-inch chain. There he was left for days without food or water while the owner worked at a nursing home. He was rescued when neighbors complained to the County Attorney. That he survived and came into our purview as a lively, bouncy animal who craved attention and affection and pushed other dogs out of the way to get it is also not reflected in the story, but is true nonetheless. It is also true that he was a short time away from being euthanized by the local humane association.

In *The Horse That Cried,* there was a genuine friendship between Lonesome Dart and his friend, Tribute. When Tribute was a pup, the two animals bonded. What is not revealed is that Lonesome Dart was originally bred as a Standardbred race horse and was not to be kept as a pet but to be sold as a Pacer. His dam earned well over $160,000. His half brother earned over $100,000 and indeed, Lonesome could have fetched a handsome amount at any legitimate sale because his sire, dam and half brother all raced successfully. He was not sold though, in part due to the fact that his brother had not commanded much attention at his sale and the agent who sold him for us did little to make him more attractive. Primarily though, after we sold Lonesome's half brother, we felt criminalized as if we had sold one of our very own children. We never escaped that feeling and thus, we could not bring ourselves to sell Lonesome Dart. That the racing world lost the better of the two horses is also not reflected in my stories. The focus was on the friendship of Lonesome Dart and Tribute.

What is also not disclosed is that *The Horse That Cried* was my very first published work. This version is much longer and more intense than the previous work but is just as true. As I write this Introduction, Lonesome Dart has suffered blindness in one eye and may in fact lose sight in the other eye. Perhaps, it is destined that he joins his friend Tribute. If so, it is my only consolation as I have come to love the horse I detested. He has come to trust and rely on me. The reader will note the similarity of facts in *The Horse That Cried* and *The Long Shot Dog.* I am writing of the same animals; only the perspective changes. In the former story, the focus is on Tribute and his friend, Lonesome Dart. It deals with the horse's sentiments at losing his friend. In *The Long Shot Dog,* the focus centers on my final relationship with Tribute.

Our Doberman, Nikki, inspired *The Ghost Beside Me.* Animal friends come and go. Some, for various reasons, remain outstanding in our minds. Nikki enjoyed a shallow pool near the point where our road joined Woods Creek. She wallowed in it whenever she was walked down the road. Sad to say, when County water was installed it was necessary to re-grade the creek and thus her pool is no more. Sometimes as I pass by the woods, I hear her ask: "What have they done with my pool?" I have no answer because progress has no reply.

Her son, Tribute, gave rise to the story *Long Shot Dog.* We purchased Nikki strictly only for breeding purposes. My own dog, Taurus, was failing and Nikki was his last chance to enjoy breeding rights and to sire an offspring. No one believed this would come about. Taurus and I did.

When Tribute was grown and had to relieve himself, he picked up a pillow and carried it around in his mouth. This he deposited at the door when we leashed him for his walk. On his return, he returned the pillow in its original place on the couch. Today, when I see this same pillow, it's hard not to choke up. Part of his spirit still resonates there.

In *The Crooked Horse,* there is some poetic license taken. We never rode Frenzy and therefore she was not one of our trail horses. What is not revealed was my wife's love and caring for an old mare who was bred until she could breed no longer and then abandoned. What is not revealed is the special bond that existed between two females, two mothers, Frenzy and Virginia. When Frenzy became so infirm she could not balance herself to be shod, my wife resorted to countless means after means to level her feet so she could walk more comfortably. Imagine my chagrin when I returned home one day to find the farrier and my wife lying side by side in a field, Virginia holding the mare's leg while Frenzy lay on her side, the farrier trimming and shaping the foot.

Those who cared for her were not bad people and I hope I do not imply that they were. On the contrary, they did their best. She was the responsibility of those who profited from her and they disclaimed that liability. They were the poorer for it and we, the richer. There are times I see her standing by the copse where she is buried. Times I wonder if urging her to stand was the right thing to do. I was not cruel in the way I tapped her with the towel. Still, I hope she understood I was fighting death, not her.

Those who think that *Talking Horse* had a sad ending would be enlightened to know that the ending was not sad at all. Willie is alive and well and doing just fine. The point is that sometimes we have to part with an animal friend in order to find happiness for him. While that is always sad, it illustrates that every animal bond has a unique flavor both individual and special, a bond which exists only between animal and human. Willie and I loved each other. Loving a twelve hundred pound animal can be good or bad provided the human understands the true needs of the horse. If he does, they can be herd mates. If he doesn't then he can, as I have done, find his way to the hospital on three occasions with broken bones. There is a difference between a horse that loves you and one that respects you. That little piece of information cost me innumerable hurts and harms. I hope it spares you if you are a horse person who doesn't know the difference.

The Cardinal is perhaps the only story where I focused on myself somewhat but that is to give inspiration to those who lose their friends and need another. There is hope… for all of us. I truly believe Nikki came back as a red cardinal, to comfort me, to give me purpose and to say she was well and free. It is also a message for those who carry the burden of personal anger. My treatment of Virginia was unpardonable. I needed a very good book and a diminutive cardinal to teach me that. Hopefully a study of the topic will aid you as well, dear reader, because I just don't think there are all that many messenger cardinals flying around giving inspiration.

As to *The Return of Lucky,* some of the story is fictional in that Lucky and I dreamed of many trail rides but the only trail ride we enjoyed alone was described in this story. Mom generally would not let me out of her sight. That's the reason he and I hit the trail early in the morning. That we both became ill as a result is true. That Lucky died of pneumonia while I fought for my life is also true. What I hope is true is that in the afterworld, Lucky is waiting for me, along with my other animal friends. Surely, Heaven must be vast enough that we can be rejoined with those we loved in life! Could our God be so unfair as to teach us love, and then, deprive us?

And thus I depart, having labored through this Introduction only because it is customary to do so. I sincerely hope you enjoy my first effort. I did not write it for money, although recovering my costs or making a profit would certainly be a welcome endorsement. But if the book makes you laugh on a day you would not otherwise laugh, if it brings a tear to your sympathetic soul, if it entertains you at a time when illness or adversity make you low, if it brings more appreciation for your own animal friends, then I have succeeded. And after all this is their story, told so they will truly become immortal.

Tears and Tales

What is the recurrent theme in my stories? Love. That a minute of the comfort and love an animal can bring is worth all the heartache, that the loyalty of an animal is endless, that from animals we can learn the simplicity of caring.

Russell A. Vassallo

April 2005

Git

A rainy mist blanched the darkening land as she descended from the truck with the all too familiar "Git". The man always spoke harshly as he had when he commanded her into the truck. She had not wanted to leave the squirming mass of life she called her puppies for it had been warm and comfortable with them and their tiny squealing brought happiness to her face. Now, as GIT exited the truck the wind brushing through high trees that sloped to the road, she wondered how long it would be before she saw them again. She did not know that they were already loaded into a plastic sack and tossed mewing and wriggling into a garbage pile. In time the wriggling would stop and then the mewing and the sack would lay motionless in the refuse. But she did not know that.

Nor did she know why neither the man nor the boy looked back as the pick up motored away, belching its black smoke into the damp air. Dutifully she trotted after the truck as she had so often on the farm where she was born. A failed gun dog, frightened by gunfire, run over by the man's tractor and left to heal on her own, she learned respect and fear for the man at a young age. Yet, she loved and forgave the boy who pelted her with stones and the man who kicked her out of the way. She knew there must be kind people in the world because she had seen other animals with their human friends. They were not mean or vicious. Thus she trusted the man and the boy hoping she would one day receive the affection and praise she craved.

So when the boy ordered her away from her puppies and out the door she surmised only that she must obey, putting her trust in those unworthy of that trust. But she did not know that then.

The truck drove slowly away. She trotted behind. Trotted without question and with the loyalty inherent in her breed. And that breed was questionable, but sported some Retriever, some Border Collie and perhaps the remnants of Beagle. She was truly beautiful when she stood with upraised front paw, motionless before a hidden bird. But now she trotted behind, picking up the pace as the truck moved more quickly away from her. Then the panic as it surged away, gathering speed and moving out of her life, out of the lives of her pups. Weakened by giving birth with no care or medical aid, she soon faltered, finding herself on a quiet road with only the wind filled trees and the forbidding woods for companionship.

She lay in the road until a vehicle came. Hopefully, she snapped alert, believing the man and boy had returned. But the headlights only illuminated a tiny white dog, with cinnamon brown patches over her face and body, teats hanging low from recent birth and a hopeful face believing that her owners had returned for her. The car passed her by and she stood wonderingly, painfully disappointed that she was alone. Her human family had abandoned her.

Off to her left ran the fields that flanked the tree line.

It was dark and the mist made it darker still. Raindrops soaked her long white hairs, making her appear drab and disheveled. The field stretched out before her. She waited a very long time. And in that time cars and trucks came and went. None contained the man and the boy.

In desperation she paced into the fields and lay down to wait but when dawn streaked the eastern horizon with light, she was still abandoned. Sometimes the man commanded her to stay at the edge of the field. Perhaps that is what he was doing now. He always returned and always commanded with a gravely voice to "git" in the truck, and she always complied obediently. By her nature she was docile, frequently rolling over on her back to signify surrender and friendship. For animals which are non-aggressive, this is a sign of submission and she had survived more than one battle with other dogs because of her gentle nature.

Desperation seized her. That instinct, which is inherent in all mothers and even in the things of nature, alerted her that her puppies were hungry and needed to suckle. She circled the road, picking up the truck's scent and tracked along the country road. Tracking, sniffing, gaining scent, then losing it again, she wandered along the roadway until exhausted. She ended her thirst by dawn's light at a glittering brook whose voice shattered the choir of tree frogs and cicadas. For the first time she realized she was hungry. For the first time she was lonely.

What crime had she committed to be left along the roadway, abandoned and without her pups? After all, what had she really asked of them? That she have a warm place in the barn, curled in her corner hay bed? That she have food and water in return for her work? She wondered as only dogs can wonder. She had never known kindness at her home, not from the man, nor from the boy nor the woman. Not even the other animals there accorded her any kindness. It was an angry home filled with angry inhabitants. But it was home. It was where she nursed her pups and felt useful. In the mornings when the barn door was opened, she sallied outside to bark at the world and announce her presence. She was watchdog, companion, cattle herder and even supplied most of her own food, so why had they removed her from her pups and brought her to this lonely place?

When she lay weary and hungry along the roadside, stillness descended over the woods, fields and highway alike. She lay there until nightfall. A somber moon rose up through dark clouds. The grass hushed before the wind and lay still. She was alone then with her thoughts, simple thoughts, of a warm paper bed with squalling, whining pups waiting to be nursed as they stumbled blindly about until her teats were found. And others, clambering over one another in their blindness, searching for the food that is life.

It was before dawn when she moved, motivated by hunger. She drank again from the stream, then searched for food. Her early experience taught her to feed herself because food was hard to come by with the man and boy. Sometimes, though, the woman fed her table scraps. Not often, but sometimes.

There was no woman now, nor any table scraps. She scented the air. Something familiar wafted on the currents. Perhaps it was a fire, and fire could mean food. She trotted toward the scent, stopping every so often to check her direction. Then there it was, off in a small unfenced field, just a shanty hastily thrown together out of fresh-hewn wood and aging along with the land. A wisp of smoke puffed up from the chimney and with it came the smell of cooking food. Perhaps there would be a kind person to give her food.

"Lard a mercy," she heard the woman say, "y'all look like a bandit with that brown patch over one eye. Half starved too. I dare not feed ya' though. Pa won't like it. He shoots dogs. So scat."

She stood her ground cautiously, sensing something in the woman that made her unafraid. As dogs went she was not especially brave nor was she powerful enough to stand against other dogs except when her very existence was threatened. She gazed quietly at the woman, hoping for some small morsel of food, anything to placate her growing hunger.

Snap! Crack! She felt the lash of the man's rope as he scourged her from behind. She shot off the porch, racing for the protection of the woods, waiting for the boom to come, for she had heard gunfire before. But there were no gunshots. She slunk down into the grass and crawled away, taking no time to lick the welts. Finding the road again she trailed along the ditches on either side. Cover was her only asset. By her wits she had survived. By her wits she might survive again. Hunger forgotten, she took up the scent again but the traffic that had passed all but obliterated the one scent she sought. She plodded along the rural road. She understood then that she would never find her home or her pups. But she would never stop searching. As animals can think, she wondered whether there was any kindness in her cold world. Was there someone who might praise her, offer affection, comfort, a secure place? She was not cynical enough to lose hope. Somewhere there was someone who would treat her kindly.

She wondered why the man had struck her. What had she done? The other man had struck and kicked her too, often for no reason at all. Were all men like that? Surely she must have wondered if this were so. If so, she'd be less trusting in the future.

She stopped to survey each home she passed. None looked familiar. Nor did the landscape. She was a young dog, sixteen months or so and she had seen only what she could see when they took her in the truck. She loved to travel, loved to sit in the center seat, intent on the roadway, each new thing an object of excitement.

The sky clouded over and the misting rain began again. Nearer the creeks the mist turned to fog but she traipsed steadily along almost as if she knew where she was going. But she did not. She had never seen this landscape before. It was a lonely, deserted road, spotted with old houses that were weathered and gray with age. People built only what space they needed, added on as need dictated and abandoned the building when it could not be expanded. Shutters hung down and slanted at odd angles while roofs sagged and bent under the weight of age. When they leaned so precariously they were apt to tumble over, they were abandoned and a newer home built. In time the newer home looked almost as forlorn as the old one. Time moved on again until weed and growth overtook them all. Then they stood alone, cheerless but occupied, as though no one had ever inhabited them.

She slaked her thirst in a nearby puddle but it did not slake her hunger and that was on her again. When had she eaten last? She wondered. Perhaps two or three days. It seemed the food had stopped right after the birth of her pups when she needed it most. And now there was a savage ache in her stomach that demanded sustenance.

All day she had circled and wandered, picking up one scent, then another, pressing her long, narrow snout to the ground and fending off the heavier rainfall by hiding under trees. Then nightfall again. Her hunger was desperate. She'd chased some field mice but was too feeble to catch them. Her only choice was to steal.

She gaited along the road, searching for a source of food. A place with other animals would have food but it would also be dangerous for other animals defended their food and sounded alarms and she'd no desire to be shot at again or struck with rope. She spotted a likely place and stalked off into the high grass. It was an old house, with an old Basset Hound laying on the porch with little enthusiasm. Beside it lay a full bowl of gruelish food. There were humans there too. Perhaps they were friendly. Perhaps she might find a comfortable place to stay and they would be kind to her.

Should she casually walk up and test the old dog? Or should she wait and see if it was an inside dog? There was little enough activity. The people put on the lights, for darkness came early these days but no one came out.

Patiently she waited, the hunger chewing at her insides like a fire fighting to be free. But she'd learned patience because impatience brought her the man's boot if she dared approach any food. The night turned cool and the Hound lay so very still that she thought it dead.

Just when she resolved to approach, it rose, circled and lay down again. Restless. In a fair fight she could easily have beaten the animal but she was not inclined to fight. Her retriever lineage made her docile and tractable and she fought only for protection of herself or her food.

As time dragged, she fell asleep. When she awoke the Basset Hound was gone and the lights had blinked into darkness. She rose quietly, stealthed her way to the front porch and stood standing stark still, listening, scenting, moving her eyes from side to side. No movement. Not anywhere. She padded softly forward, stopped, watched, listened again. She hugged close to the ground and inched forward as though some primeval instinct drove her to be cautious. An inch, another, across the front lawn, now at the foot of the porch. Should she stop and feed her fill? Or should she steal a mouthful and race away? She was weary and wanted a place to rest. Could she risk staying only to find they were unkind to her?

A light surged on. She froze. Suddenly the front door opened and the Basset Hound emerged and waddled down the front steps. It stopped and stared at the ragged intruder. The visitor emitted a menacing growl. The Hound scurried quickly by, relieved itself and raced to the front door which opened and engulfed him.

She ate with trepidation for she was not unused to the man booting her out of the way so his coon hounds could eat first. When they were done, there was little left and she was forced to forage for food. Mice, voles, an occasional rabbit or squirrel. Thus she ate quickly, tensely as if every bite might be her last. At the farm where she was born, the man and boy kicked her away from the food until the hunting dogs had eaten. She learned to be wary and suspicious. If the other dogs caught her eating, they stole the food from her.

There were few leaves on the trees as she cut through the darkness. Somewhere, she knew, there would be shelter. An old building, a copse of cedar trees, somewhere away from the cold of the creeks. Then she rested, licking her paws until she fell into a fitful sleep. In her sleep she dreamed, bolted and shook awake. She prowled then through the night, seeking a more restful shelter, for the evening had turned cold.

Through a stand of shagbark hickory she saw a dilapidated building and approached it. It was abandoned. It reeked of age and urine, swine and fowl and it was porous and broken like a haunted spirit from which the life had been sapped. But it was shelter from the wind and so she curled into a desperate sleep against an inner wall.

She started awake with the smell of flame and smoke and shouting. Sparks crackled through the air, landing on her back. She could smell her long hair singeing. In moments the entire building flamed with fire. Great sparks blew in wind swept curls. The door through which she had come was now engulfed in flame. She heard voices and barked at the sound. When she next looked up, the entire roof was on fire. Water was careening off the rafters and sizzling on the burning wood and the withered roof was disintegrating in huge chunks of flame. In panic, she leapt through the flaming door into the air outside. But there were men there. Firemen. Men who practiced fire control and often used old buildings for their work. She darted into the woods still howling and raced off into the forest. She had missed one appointment with destiny and yet she had met another.

She traveled for miles, putting the fire behind her, more lost now than ever. She doubted she'd ever see her pups again but it did not daunt her spirit. She would keep looking. On and on she trotted through hollows, up ridges, through stands of oak and buckeye and then through swamps laced with cedar and yellow poplar. She did not ask much. Only to find her pups and raise them. Only to have a home where she found love and not abuse. Now, her pups were gone. Her home was gone.

It was nightfall again and she was on another country road. There were few homes but one, distant from the roadway, still shone. She crossed the creek and followed the road, keeping to the shadows. She had not eaten all day and the road seemed to lead to the only house along the way. Something moved by the great house. She halted abruptly.

A tiger striped cat bent low to its food and quietly ate, then full, wandered off and became a mere shadow as it disappeared. There was food remaining in the dish. The diminutive dog could see that. Tiny crumbled food that smelled of fish. She did not care. Food was survival and if she was to find her way home, she needed sustenance. Still, she crept slowly, a step here, then stop, another step or two, expecting any moment the brutal kick that always came.

She inhaled every crumb and licked the plate for the last of the nourishment. She did not know when she would find another meal. There was water there too but she preferred the cool running water of the creeks. She slipped quietly into the darkness and back to the roadway where a garbage box lay. And there, she bedded down for the night.

At sunrise, a passing car awoke her, leaving from the house where she had eaten. The man glanced at her curiously as he drove by. He said nothing but neither did he stop to chase her away. There was the scent of dogs on his vehicle. She would have to be careful if she went there again to eat. She was a small dog and in her weakened condition she was no match for any size animal, let alone more than one.

That evening, under a darkening sky, she crept close to the house again. The cat was not there but the man she had seen earlier was working outside. She thought of approaching him but he was a man and she had not been treated kindly by men. So she waited in the shadows again and when he had gone, she stalked the food as would a wild animal. Each sound startled her to readiness. Each mouthful alerted her to danger. But it was food and she was grateful to find it.

When morning came she was camped again by the garbage box. Often there was something carelessly thrown out that she could eat. She saw the man again, several times that day but he did nothing more than glance at her. For days the same scene played out again and again. She waited out the daylight hours hunting the nearby fields for anything she could eat. Then wearied from her efforts, she awaited nightfall when she could steal food from the dish near the house.

But this time, when she approached she heard voices. A man and woman were talking. She did not understand the words but she sensed they were discussing the missing cat food. She sensed in the people a kindness or at least an absence of anger and briefly considered approaching them and showing submissiveness. Hungry though she was, it was too risky to expose herself to these humans, even by pilfering. Quietly, she retreated into the shadows, miserable and cold, hunger striking at her very soul. She hunkered down along the road, waiting for the lights to go out but they did not. It would be another foodless night, another night chasing sounds in the grass and catching nothing, another night curling into a small, round shield against the cold wind. She wondered if she just should lay there until Death came. Would it not be simpler than dying a little each day? Though small, she was courageous and determined. Tomorrow, perhaps, she might find kindness and love. Perhaps even a pup to nurture.

She had forgotten how she arrived at this place. She had raced from the fire in panic and fear of the shouting men and had cut through forests of poplar and beech, keeping the trees between her and the men so they could not trace her retreat. When she reached the creek, she stepped into it and followed it for a long time until it deepened. As a retriever she could easily have swum but she was panting for breath and exhausted from her escape.

She wandered about now, trying again to catch the scent of her home, something, anything that would bring her back to her pups. She failed and having failed, gave a soft whimper and lay down in the tall grass to preserve her body heat. A bright moon mounted the high ridges. The light gave her hope. It was a clear and frosty night, one she gladly would have traded for warm, soft bedding. Straw or hay that generated heat would have suited her. But she had none. She arose and trotted down the long, dark road to the house again. The lights were on but no one was about. There was a cat bed lying alongside the food dish. It looked comfortable and inviting. She could sleep there and leave before early light. She retreated again to the shadows and waited to see if anything came for the food. One by one the house lights were extinguished until it lay in silent darkness. She stalked off into the fields, recalling that she had often found field mice or rabbits scampering about in late evening. She was fortunate enough to trap a mouse beneath her paw, almost by accident. She had taken up residence by the garbage box near the road and thus she returned there.

But she was not alone. Something growled near the place where she usually lay. It had torn open a plastic garbage bag and was searching for food. After the first growl came a second, further to the right of her and then another, just behind her. She was encircled. Coyotes. Perhaps wild dogs. She felt a nip on her right leg but did not turn to defend herself. These were hungry animals. Animals that would kill and eat anything in their path. Instinctively, she wheeled and raced away. They pursued her. Fast, agile, they were fast. She was faster. She wheeled and dodged and raced straight away, leaving them just behind her. They were agile and fast, better able to run a distance. If she were to escape, it needed to be soon for she was already tired.

A house loomed up. The chase set their own dogs to barking. A German Shepherd charged down into the fray, passing the female and heading directly toward the pursuers. They stopped abruptly and stood snarling at the Shepherd. Another dog charged from the house, also passing her and heading for the trespassers. They were bristling for a fight she had no stomach for. While the animals held each other at bay, she quietly circled around and returned to the darkness near the man's house.

The cat bed was empty but she dared not risk sleeping there. Instead she selected a windless place near the barn, disturbed only by the grazing horses that also resided there. Near morning, she went in search of food and stopped near the garbage box. As the man passed this day, he slowed his vehicle and spoke to her from the window. His voice sounded kind and reassuring. She approached the vehicle but he slowly crept forward and left. And each day on his leaving and return, he stopped to speak with her and she became more confident of him.

Finally, she approached the house, determined to find the man, to seek some kindness from him. It was early evening. The huge garage door was open and the man descended the stairs within, carrying something large in his arms. It was a dog which he held in his arms and laid gently on the tail gate of his pickup. The man's animal did not move and she smelled Death and knew the large dog was cold and lifeless. And then he made a whimpering sound, such as she had made when thinking of her puppies. She heard the voice of human misery, understood the depth of his love. She wanted to comfort the man but she did not know how. The man remained for a very long time before driving the dead animal to a nearby place on the farm. There, he laid the animal into the ground and covered it over with dirt. She again heard the voice of misery, was near enough to see the wetness on his face. After he left, she did not follow but lay upon the grave. The man had lost his puppy and motherly instincts appointed her to guard it. Night after night, she pilfered the cat food. Night after night she guarded the grave. She understood now why she had come here, understood her role to console the man. He did not comprehend this now, but no matter, it would come in time. The man no longer spoke to her as he passed her normal haunt. In time, when his dog did not come from beneath the earth, she abandoned her post, convinced the puppy was gone. So she remained by the garbage box, surviving as she could.

Each day, the man passed. He looked sad and empty now and seldom glanced in her direction. Each day, she went to the house searching for food. Each day she visited the grave, growing weaker. Each night she purloined what little food was left. She was wretchedly starved now. Her teats hung down where milk had long ago dried. Her narrow face seemed hopeless, almost desperate. Earlier and earlier she came to search for food for there was nothing in the fields she could catch. The neighboring dogs jealously guarded their own dinners and when she approached their territory, they warned her off.

In frantic desperation, she straggled up the long, steep driveway one evening, almost too weary to make the high grade. Then startled, she saw the man standing by the house, staring at her. Something in the man said he needed her but something else said he was unaccepting. Still, he did not chase her. Nor did he yell "git". She saw something in his eyes. Perhaps fate had led her here, here to this pup that needed her. Here to a place that was home.

Her eyes roamed from man to food dish and to man again. "Ah," he muttered "so you're the possum stealing my cat food."

Then he made a motion she had seen so many times before, a motion that a raised arm was about to strike, to chase her off.

Instead he brushed back his gray hair and stared at her. Her own eyes were soft and pleading. The man shifted his eyes upward.

"Lord, I know I'm making a mistake," he said," and disappeared into the garage. She stood puzzled, unsure of her next move.

He appeared again; this time the dish was full. Her face brightened at the sight of food but she approached slowly.

"I do not want another dog," the man said. She heard him but did not understand the irritation in his voice.

"I just lost my greatest friend. No one can replace him," he said before he set the food down. She gazed at him quietly, her eyes watching his every move.

"You can eat and then stay in the cat bed until tomorrow and then you git." He continued staring at her, noting the shriveled teats hanging down, the crooked angle of her right rear leg, the crusted dirt on her underbelly. He shook his head and pushed the food dish closer with his foot. She advanced and began eating.

"But you look so ragged. Did they turn you loose to shift on your own? Did they not care if you lived or died? And what did they do with your pups? Did they take them or did the coyotes? Well, perhaps you can stay a while until you're stronger." He crouched and motioned her to advance. She did so cautiously. So often had she been battered when eating that when he knelt to pet her, she scurried away. She did not understand, nor did he. But his voice was soft and reassuring and she returned again to eat.

"You look a sight," he murmured. "Never saw a dog so wretched. I thought you belonged to a neighbor and wondered who."

She eyed him again but ate the food slowly, delicately. When finished she stepped toward him, slowly lowered her body until it touched the ground. Then she rolled on her back, her stomach exposed in the supreme sign of trust and submission to the alpha male. He was hurting from the loss of his dog. He did not want a replacement. As he gazed into her eyes he saw they were kind and loving. A voice within him whispered that this little brown and white, ragged animal was not there to replace his lost friend. She was there to ease his pain. She was there to follow along by his side. She was there to lay her head on his lap as they sat in the living room. She was there to alert him to strangers coming onto the property. She was there to be his friend. Perhaps his guardian angel sent her. A do over. Not a replacement because nothing could replace the love in his heart he felt for his lost friend. But a beginning. A new beginning just as life is full of new beginnings. All he had to do was try.

He smiled, rubbed her stomach, shook his head sadly, then quickly disappeared into the garage. The door shut. The light went out. Weary, she turned to the cat bed and curled into a tiny ball. She sighed, for tonight she would be safe and warm. She thought of her puppies, her former home but the man here seemed to need her. He seemed so sad and alone. In time, she would accept that her puppies were gone. And in time, the man would accept her. Perhaps like the others he would say “git” and mean it but she did not think so. She sensed some inner kindness in the man and she had survived by sensing such things. Perhaps he would let her stay. Yes, something in the man said he needed her. She had suffered abandonment only to find a new home, a good home. Fate had hurt her only to lead her to happiness. In a way she had found her pup and now all she had to do was grow strong and raise him.

She snuggled deeper into the cat bed and tightened her curl against the night air. With a long, deep sigh, she closed her eyes. Tomorrow. Tomorrow, she would help him herd the horses and run alongside him as he walked. She’d guard him, point birds that hid in the fields, raising one front leg as she stood. The man would shoot them and she’d retrieve them, for that was her breeding. For this man she’d overcome her fear of gunfire. Yes, she could do that. When the work was done, she’d return to her bed, to her home. He was her pup. She had to care for him because he much needed that care. And she needed a home.

Home. Yes, home.

It had a very nice ring, comforting and secure.

HOME.

The Ghost Beside Me

A ghost walks beside me, slipping quietly into the woods beyond. Other times, she wades stomach deep in the bend of the silver creek where a pool has formed. But always she is with me, in my thoughts, my heart, in the very substance that makes life meaningful and full. She was real once. Flesh and blood. Not always a ghost. No, once she was just an ad in the newspaper that read:

FOR SALE: female Doberman, age three, registered and papers, nice disposition $75.00.

We were looking for a mate to our aging Doberman, Taurus. Something about him that followed me into retirement drove me to perpetuate him. If I could have cloned him I would have, but only because I was lost in a new State, without the shield of my law practice, without the protectiveness of being a useful parent, without much purpose at all. My wife, our trail horses, the hills and ridges around us, the beauty of Fall colors, the quiet creeks that bordered us, the freedom to do with my time what I pleased, all should have been enough. But they were not. I needed something of Taurus because he was the only remaining vestige of what I once had been. My life had been an active one, lawyer, father, defender of the oppressed. My roots originated in Newark, a metropolitan area with thousands of people, traffic, noise and pollution. What I thought would be an escape to Heaven became a prison of depression and sadness. I could not adjust to doing nothing, to being nothing. It was not that I had nothing to do for there was much to do on the farm. The depression sprang from poor self image. I needed to be needed. I needed to feel secure in the authority I had both as lawyer and as father. When I abandoned these things to settle in rural America, stripped of my power as a lawyer, devoid of my responsibility as a father, raising a step son who used his mother's love as a weapon against my authority, I sank into a meaningless life. Depression became my partner.

Suicide became my goal. Without an offspring from Taurus, I felt I would be completely abandoned.

So I jumped when I saw the ad. Seventy-five dollars was unheard of for a female Doberman. We drove to the distant farm where that secret bargain lay. And when an old oaken stable door slid heavily open, my wife and I peered into impenetrable darkness, a gloom so vast it shocked us to think that anything lived there. And what emerged from that stable, charging into the sunlight with eyes blinking from the darkness was a short, robust, black and tan female with badly cropped ears and short black hair. She was encrusted with manure but wore a bright, empty smile nonetheless. She peered past us as if we did not exist and started to wander until her mistress commanded her to stay. Only then did she become aware of us.

Nikki was a strange dog. She had the vacant stare of a retarded child, distant and detached but her eyes seemed to exert her will in a soft, searching, quizzical way. That she had been used as a mere breeding machine was obvious from her low slung teats and thick waist. That she was the runt of the litter was apparent from her short stature.

This was Princess Nikki Eversole. Not much on royalty, I thought and wavered in my resolve to purchase her. I think, though, it was her brown motherly eyes that captivated me. Or perhaps it was the simpleton smile. Whatever it was, something dictated she should not be sent back into that gloom to languish in manure while she awaited the next buyer.

Nikki was one of fourteen Dobes indiscriminately owned by an old, uncaring farmer who bred in volume and sold cheaply. Her ears had been poorly cropped and her tail docked too long but she was not unattractive. I suspect the farmer had done the work himself. When he died his daughter inherited the dogs. Not having room for more than two, she was selling most of them. My own plans for Nikki were no better. She was to be bred to our Taurus and then sold or given away, so it mattered little what she looked like. I needed some remnant of Taurus because he was dying and I just could not let him go. But I did not need Nikki and her fate would not concern me. I would not let myself love because love hurts. As Evita Peron said, "You keep your distance."

Nikki accepted life on its own terms and with stoicism. She jumped into the front seat of our pickup as though she had been there before or knew that we were destined to befriend her. Though she bonded with my wife, Virginia, she distrusted me. For months I feared some wrong move would cause her to attack. But she never did. Still, if I shifted my leg while sitting, or raised a swatter to hit a fly, Nikki skittered away. She could not speak, yet she spoke of her past and her life with the farmer. There would come a time when I could stroke her stomach with my bare foot or even play with her, but that would be in the distant future. Nikki did not know she was a dog. Or she did not know we were people. It would be months before she played with Taurus as dogs will play. She simply did not know how. When she did, she and Taurus would stare each other down, creep slowly toward one another, and then clash in mock battle. Nikki swooped low, feinted right, then left, then right, then lunged forward plowing into Taurus with her full weight. She was learning dog play from Taurus, but if I held a pull toy in front of her she looked dumbly at it and backed away.

In shock I watched as Virginia dropped to all fours, crept slowly forward, then stared directly into Nikki's eyes. Eye to eye contact with an animal is often a sign of aggression and will cause the other to attack.

"Virginia," I started, "that's asking for trouble. Dogs regard eye to eye contact as prefacing an attack."

"No, love. She's not vicious, inside she's just a little child. She's full grown outside. A baby inside. She just doesn't know what to do."

And typical of the wisdom of all women, Nikki responded by playing with her. In time she learned that when I offered her a pull toy it was a game, not a punishment and then she played vigorously, tugging with all her might. For a small dog she was amazingly strong.

If there was any manner of approach to Nikki it was food. She was an Epicurean. So when I ate she would gently slide her snout at table's edge, imploring eyes plied back and forth from food to my eyes. And who could deny those expressive, pleading, all knowing eyes? She plied her female charms on an obedient servant until he submitted. Then, she did not savage the food but mouthed it sensitively as though uncertain until the last moment that it was hers and then she ate slowly, patiently and returned only after a respectable lapse. But although the bond grew between her and Virginia, two females taking walks, playing dog games, nestled together on the couch watching television, only a cautious friendship emerged between Nikki and me. If there were any plateau on which I could approach Nikki, it was her love of food and food alone. Whatever her level of thought, Nikki held a distrust of men.

Nikki was bred to Taurus, not that Virginia and I had anything to do with nature following a prescribed course, for we did not.

Nikki and Taurus found their own pleasure and Nikki became pregnant. She did not announce her time. Instead she went to the couch where she slept, proceeded to dig a hole in the cushion, and had five pups, only one of which survived. Because I was a man and ignorant of a mother's feelings, I removed each dead pup and buried it without a single thought to her. From the whimpering cries, I later understood that pups had been removed from her before and probably with as little consideration. It was as though I had punished her for some unknown crime. In truth I felt defenseless about the death of each puppy and could never find human words to console her. But even now, I hear her pitiful cries as I removed each dead puppy to bury it.

As a symbol of her love, she never exacted any revenge but tried in her simplistic way to trust and to understand why I had done so. Nor did she ever cease searching for them. We could never show a video of her puppies without her racing frantically about the house as the tiny squeals of her puppies played back on the tape. It was pitiable to watch her desperately searching the V.C.R. or the speakers or sniffing and circling the television, time and again, trying to locate her missing pups. Such is motherhood that hope never dies or the memory of a missing offspring fade.

She raised the surviving puppy, Tribute. She taught him. What she lacked in intelligence, she commuted with instinct and sweetness. Yet, she had three bites to her credit. One to my son, Russell, who did nothing to threaten or offend her but who, in my opinion, deserved a bite on general principles. One to a hired man who tried to pass her station at our bedroom door and finally an old friend who had seen and petted her many times but was approaching Virginia and therefore was a danger. On yet another occasion she permitted a salesman to enter the house but refused to let him leave, holding him with her low, insidious snarl while drawing back her upper lip over savage, white fangs. In her time she chased off the gas man, the U.P.S. driver and several Jehovah's Witnesses— the latter with my complete approval.

She trotted the woodland trails with Virginia and developed favorite haunts, especially a low pool in the creek where in summer she wallowed. I never feared for Virginia when Nikki was with her. On more than one occasion she charged me until she heard my voice and recognized me. And on each such occasion I vowed to get rid of her once the pup was raised. Fate was to govern my actions though.

Across from our house is the well field, so called because our well is sunk there. It was there that she and Virginia were surrounded by a wild dog pack. I heard the commotion of Nikki fending them off, snarling and snapping as each one approached. I had never seen anything so fierce and wild. Nor have I seen a dog with such primeval instincts for survival. With one dog confronting her and two behind her, Nikki charged the leader, a big, silver-black Shepherd with blazing eyes and long, ugly incisors. He braced for the attack while the smaller dogs lay in from behind. Without warning, Nikki wheeled and savaged the smaller dog to her left, tearing huge chunks of skin from its snout. Before they could down her I arrived, shot one and wounded another. The remaining dogs raced down the creek, leaving their fallen comrade to die. After that there was no talk of selling her.

My lingering depression did not improve nor did Nikki have any impact on me with her distrust of men. Although she freely accepted food from me, there tarried an untrusting reserve, that there were too many years of flailings and indiscriminate kicks simply to be forgotten. She accepted my commands with resignation but her affections clearly lay with Virginia. It was this distrust that depressed me even further. My grown children had been left behind in New Jersey, well able to fend for themselves and yet, the gnawing guilt that I had abandoned my responsibility to them remained. I did not need the further rejection of a mere dog, one so much a failure that she did not resemble any well bred Doberman I had ever seen. Perhaps she made me feel more useless than I already felt as a parent. I do not know. I only know that a distance remained between us that was unsettling.

I often spoke to Virginia about our original plan to sell her. But even as I said the words I knew I would not have the heart to part with her. Perhaps I recalled the vivid guilt of my first Dobe, Poco, caught in the battle of divorce, the innocent victim of a vengeful wife and my neglect. Whatever the cause, Poco suffered a stroke and in my agony and grief, I could find no solution for her pain. She lay in the vet's office waiting for me to come. But I had separated and had no room in my quarters for her. My office was not my own. I lived in an apartment with a woman not my wife. Without me, on whom she lavished her affection, Poco quickly faded and passed away. Wherever she is I am certain she has forgiven me. But for me, Poco was a casualty that inflicts heavy guilt for my sin of neglect and I have never forgiven myself. Nothing of Nikki resembled Poco, yet she reminded me of my guilt. So Nikki stayed and the restless truce continued.

It furthered our relation somewhat when Taurus lay dying on a warm front porch. That she lay quietly by his side, leaving only to eat and relieve herself demonstrated a brand of loyalty I truly admired. After his death, the depressions that plagued me all my life, intensified. There was sadness in me that denied the necessity of life. As if all knowing, Nikki kept her distance and bonded even more with Virginia. That her pup was growing and bonding with no one deepened my futility.

So she went her way with Virginia and I remained aloof and uncaring. She grew on me and I liked her but neither of us trusted the other. It was obvious she had been harshly treated, been shunned by the litter, abused by her owner, abandoned by his daughter and finally adopted by someone who cared as little about her as he did about his own life.

The standoff might have lasted forever but as always fate takes a hand and alters the outcome. Nikki failed to approach me for her evening table treat. When she took her last walk with Virginia, she was listless, her steps faltering and shaky. Her temperature was high. Her nose warm. Worst of all, the brightness in her eyes was replaced by a dull, distant resignation. I had the distinct impression Nikki had given up, much as I had. She was desperately ill.

Because of my background in hospital work, I medicated most of the animals. Virginia therefore looked to me for aid. I tried aspirin to reduce her fevers. Several times a day I drenched her with alcohol, chilling her forehead and swamping her entire body until she cooled. We pumped antibiotics into her with minimal results. What was not minimal, though, was that Nikki, for the first time was under my control and relied on me for relief. I found myself slipping under her spell, loving her and trusting her more at each session. She, too, placed herself under my care. I realized then that Nikki was not as fearful as she was lost and directionless, not so much fierce as she was frightened, not so much vicious as she was loyal.

When it became apparent this illness was not a passing thing, it was I who carried her to the car and kept an ice pack on her forehead.

Nikki was not a dog that licked your face or hands. Her affection was more human and she could say with one glance what hundreds of words might not. In her eyes I saw fear, saw the need for her to be assured. I also saw a complete resignation of will. She was stoic and resigned but determined not to leave her family. How I read that or knew that I will never know. It is just one of those things one knows with as much certainty as life itself. I stroked her head and spoke soothing words. She was fatigued from the fever but breathed a relaxed sigh. I knew then she was content and the fear was gone.

The vet conducted one test after another. The results, as they mostly are, were inconclusive. It "might" be a virus. It "might" be something she ate. It "might" be an intestinal infection. It "might" be. It might be. It might be. It might be but it never "is". Good men are perplexed by life and befuddled by death. They search among their own means for solutions and find only their own infinitesimal status within the universe. Those of good heart are saddened by this inability and yet it is no more their fault than frost upon a windowpane.

We watched through a little window as they incised her stomach, watched the oxygen pump as she breathed in and out, that little black ball showing that the life-force was still there and that her determination to stay with the family she loved was still massively strong. The vet held part of her uterus which was swollen and inflamed. He removed the ovaries which were also infected. It is a common disease in older bitches. From that we understood he had found the offending part. Later he was to tell us that in a day or two she would have been dead. But she was not. Something in that stunted little animal compelled a will to live and shamed me for all the suicidal thoughts I carried. And something in that stunted little animal remembered my kindness and bonded to me. It was a rewarding moment when she crawled between us in bed one day and snuggled comfortably there. It was as though she returned to the litter and was harbored safely within. She poked her nose under my arm and propped her stubby tail against Virginia. There she lay, content and secure.

There was a drawback to this clan-like behavior though, for Virginia and I could never answer the call of carnal lust without Nikki feeling excluded and offended. She took to howling, a long moaning, bellowing howl that began in the rear of her throat and sunk lower and lower into her abdomen. When we opened the bedroom door she charged in, casting reproachful glances at us as though we were errant children caught at bad behavior. Nikki was genuinely hurt at her exclusion. But I rather suspect that as the dominant female she fully expected to be included. It often occurred to me that the neighborhood could well be aware of our conjugal bliss if they had any inkling at all why Nikki was howling and moaning. Fortunately they did not.

As we progressed in our bonding I sensed in Nikki something more than mere animal affection, a true and simple comprehension of love. She never accepted any kindness without returning thanks in some way. She was never more secure than when cuddled between Virginia and me. She was fierce in her devotion and dedicated in her loyalty. She wanted love. She gave love. If she felt lonely or abandoned she simply nudged her nose under my hand and pushed until I rubbed her snout. She reveled in her daily walks with Virginia. She enjoyed her moments of play with us and Tribute. She nestled between us so that part of her body rested on each of us. And she terrorized anyone who came to our door. Nikki was a no nonsense guard dog and I often marveled at how docile she could be with Virginia and me and how hostile she could be with visitors. She tolerated people we admitted into the house but outside was her territory. She brooked no transgressions on her turf. With children, she became a mother again, scolding them if they played too roughly, loving them if they were kind and docile. She blossomed into something lost, then discovered, and into something which belonged.

There was a seed growing though. The seed of love, of attachment. But there was another seed growing in both of us. In me, it was a tiny seed in my colon, which would grow from normal tissue into colon cancer and would strike me some time later. In Nikki a simple and routine examination revealed lymphoma cancer, with a life expectancy of six months if we did not treat her and one year, perhaps, if we did.

Then came the million doubts and questions one asks.

What about chemotherapy? How long for her then? How will it affect her? Will it be painful? Will she be able to eat and drink?

Will she lose hair? Bladder control? How will the end come? How will we know?

In the end these are all questions no one can answer. There are no answers. Life is not definable. Nor is it certain or predictable. Weeks dragged by and treatment dragged with it. Nikki seemed no better or worse. She accepted her treatment stoically and without question, going trustingly with the vet tech who administered her chemo. She seemed neither to want to live nor to die. And yet her daily determination to survive, to do the things she loved most, taught me the humility of understanding true faith and trust in loved ones. She grew plump. Her appetite increased from the use of steroids. Even in adversity there is sometimes humor.

One evening Virginia had prepared a roast for dinner. She did it more to entice my failing appetite than for show. A few moments after she signaled dinner ready, she came up to the bedroom to assist me downstairs. She heard a cry and left me to investigate, returning moments later, half tearful, half laughing.

"How'd ya like to go out for dinner?" she smiled wanly.

"Okay by me, but I thought we were having roast."

"We were, but Nikki decided to dine alone."

Famished from the steroids which gave her an insatiable appetite, Nikki had done the unpardonable… leapt up on the table and snatched away the roast. It little mattered to me whether I ate or not. And it little mattered if the seed of pain within me grew worse. Life did not matter. But it mattered to Nikki in unfathomable ways. Her time lingered beyond the year, far beyond, to two and one half years. As sick as she was, she would not surrender. I marveled at how easily I had given up and how tenaciously she clung to the people who loved her. In her declining days she suffered a loss of bladder control. Regrettably we could no longer allow her to sleep with us and had to confine her to the pantry for naps and evening slumber. Still she did not wince. She sustained nose bleeds. We tried numerous remedies. On two occasions she endured death, fading into a coma only to be revived by Virginia's startled voice and rough shaking. I put aside the excruciating pain in my abdomen and focused only on the valiant little animal who defied death. Firm in the belief that she survived because she dared not leave us, we revived her from each seizure. In the end, though, the pain I suffered overcame me and I doubled up and lay agonized on the basement floor where Virginia found me. I could help Nikki no more and Virginia was already strained from dealing with an ailing husband, a dying dog, seven horses and several cats.

I conceded a physician was needed. I saw him. As with Nikki's testing, there were no solid answers. Only speculation. Doctors convened and arrange for hospital testing. I would go, only after convincing myself I would return home the same day. We spent the time nursing Nikki, playing with her, walking her, photographing her wading in her knee deep pool. Except for her loss of bladder control, she hardly seemed ill at all. We did not know our time clocks were ticking away like the boisterous bang of a celestial drum, beating away the heartbeats and depleting life.

I arose early that morning, still groggy from lack of sleep. It had been a disturbed and painful night. Nothing else would change. Only the hands of my own life clock would move forward. But then I heard Virginia's cry and rushed to meet her, descending the stairs with abandon until I met the reason for her cry.

Nikki, she said, had come smiling out of the pantry, greeted her one last time, and collapsed. She could not be revived. She lay stretched and unmoving on the floor, inches from her pantry home. Although Virginia called her and shook her, we both knew that even if she revived, we could no longer care for her as we had. How Virginia kept up with all the medications and routines is still a matter of mystery to me. But another clock was urgently ticking. Not in eons but in minutes. For I had an appointment at the hospital that could not be delayed. With tears streaking my face, I laid Nikki on her blanket and dragged her to the porch. I was bleeding internally and thus had not the strength to lift and carry her. I knelt beside her and stroked her one last time. My hope that I would return later that day and find her alive again never faded. Not as they prepared me for testing, not as they told me I had a tumor that had to be removed immediately, not in the recovery room when I was aroused from the sleep of death, not as I weakly mounted the stairs to my home two weeks later. There was always hope that my old friend was alive and waiting there.

She was not though. She was gone. No last moments. No time for tears. She cared for us until we could not care for her, and then she surrendered. So there was no more than cold burial, without sorrow, without mourning and thus the mourning remains a thing undone. Still more, her headstone remains unmounted because it bears a finality which is beyond me.

For that, I always hated the cancer that struck me. I raged against it. Not because it threatened my life. Life had no value for me. I hated it because cancer took my friend and cancer prevented my last goodbye. From that rage, I summoned the courage to survive. Otherwise, there would be no meaning to Nikki's life, nor any meaning to her love. But the rage subsided. In its place was the memory of a love so deep, so loyal, that my friend gave her life for me when she knew I needed care.

Whatever selfishness arises in man does not arise in animals.

Nor did it arise in Nikki. She tarried with us and fought her own battle with cancer because she loved us. Twice, we recalled her from death, because she loved us. If I permitted anger to dominate my life, to hurt those dearest to me, then her life and her death were meaningless. From this animal friend I learned to accept love, to cherish it, to live life and to mourn my lost friends. Mourn them but not with anger. Mourn them with hope that in her place will come another such friend, a friend I will be more worthy to accept.

In time I understood that love is stronger than anger. It was not anger that made me survive, but love. When I think about Nikki, I understand that every life has value, every life has purpose. As Nikki had found hers in keeping me alive, I had to find purpose

They laid her to rest with Taurus and not far from Tribute who, at six, preceded her in death by three months. There will come a time when I fashion a wooden headstone for her but it will come only when I accept her death and I let her go, as I must in order to move forward. As with all things I love, letting go is always difficult. Because she appears by her favorite wading pool, or slipping into the woods along the trails she helped forge, she can never really be gone. And so her ghost awaits me, at the shadowy transition between life and death, where all our loved ones wait, to be joined again in love.

The Horse That Cried

I didn't especially like him. In fact, I distinctly disliked him. He was pushy, arrogant and spoiled, the physical image of his racehorse dam, black in winter, liver in summer, gawky and with the same white snip dead center in his forehead. Unlike his dam that set a track record on her way to earning $160,000, he did not have the same cooperative disposition. I often described him as a four year old with the brain of an infant and despite his quaint way of trailing me all over the paddocks, I detested him. After all he repeatedly stepped on my foot.

We called him Loni although when I had higher hopes for him he was officially named Lonesome Dart. He was the only foal we imprint trained, the second foal of Dusty Dart, and an animal resolved to refuse the natural pecking order of any herd. It little mattered how often the dominant horse consigned him to his order, he nudged and pushed until he acquired equal rights to every horse's feed trough. He was balky, bull-headed and difficult to train. He worked only when he saw fit and reined whichever way he determined to go. If pushed too hard, he simply sat down and let his rider slide off his back.

He never raced but relished my wife's affection and that of his only friend our Doberman, Tribute. What Tribute saw in him escapes me but even as a pup, Tribute took an immediate liking to Loni, touching nose to nose, or slurping the big horse's face with long, wet kisses. They played at first along the fence line, Loni cantering along to keep up with Trib, then turning and racing back again. Inside the corral, Trib raced Loni end to end, skirting his great hooves and outmaneuvering him.

They made a pair, the long, slender, masculine Tribute, typical Doberman lines, alert eyes and slender snout and the gawky, often clumsy Lonesome Dart, wheeling and cavorting in the small paddock. Beyond them, the hills sloped down to the silver creek at the far fence line of the larger paddock. And when both were released into the larger field, only the wind was swifter as they hurtled toward open spaces. So Tribute would chase Loni end to end along the paddock and somewhere in the fray the tables turned and it was Loni with lowered head, charging like a bull as if to run Trib down. He never did though. As clumsy as he purported to be, he swung away at the last moment, permitting his friend to escape. Just a touch away from being caught, Trib brought the pursuit to an end and became the hunter again. One was graceful. The other was not. Yet they enjoyed a kindred bond. On more than one occasion Loni picked the lock to his paddock and paid Tribute a visit in our rear yard. Then we heard the awkward clump of hooves racing along our chain wire fencing and Trib yapping and barking in sheer ecstasy that his friend had come calling.

No, Loni was not graceful. In fact, he was a bit of a tangle foot, never knowing quite where to place his feet, slipping, tripping over himself. He had a mischievous streak in him as well. When I brought my manure spreader into the paddock to clean out the run-in shed, I found him calmly munching my tractor seat until he'd torn half the stuffing out. Days after when the jarring tractor shot sparks up my royal spine, I hated him all the more. He was totally useless and usurped the right of horses far more worthy than himself. There were Diablo and Uno, both fine trail horses and Dusty, Power Blaster and Red Leader, all fine race horses who had well earned their keep. And then there was Loni, five years old and with no significant accomplishment to call his own.

But as I walked Tribute each day, and brought him to Loni's paddock, a vexatious interplay transpired between the two animals. It was more than just two animals playing. There was chemistry between dog and horse.

So it went, from pup to adolescent, weanling to yearling, adolescent to adult, yearling to sixteen-hand horse. Whatever the relationship, Tribute gleaned some redeeming quality in Lonesome Dart, a quality I either did not see or desired to ignore. What irritated me most about Loni was his potential and how he underused it. Tribute was a guard dog and a good one. Loni was a waste. But whatever he possessed was not wasted on Tribute. They frolicked along the fence line or gazed eye to eye until one blinked and sent the other chasing. At times, Loni lay on the warm ground, bathing in sunlight and his refusal to rise would send Tribute hurtling over him as neatly as a circus dog. Then they circled, nipping at each other, Tribute grasping Loni by the tail, tugging with all his might only to be yanked off his feet and sprawled along the ground. But no matter how aggressively they played, always the play ended with a sign of affection between them. Perhaps the kindest times occurred when both animals were truly exhausted and lay side by side in the warm sun to rest. Had I not detested Lonesome Dart for his uselessness, I might have thought it cute. But I resented Trib's outward affection for an animal I deemed worthless.

Several years brought no change in their friendship except to deepen it. Nor did it wreak any change in my detestation for Lonesome Dart. I tolerated the bond because I had no choice. I could never hold Tribute well enough to keep him from yanking me toward his friend's paddock. It was simpler just to submit. Thus five years wearied on. Lonesome Dart filled out into a tall, muscular horse but he was still clumsy and no more mature than he was at two.

But Tribute remained sleek and strong and beautiful. Sometimes I put him in the back yard and I especially loved to watch him there as he faced into the wind, hair blowing straight back, with a regal stance that made him a Doberman.

Thinking back perhaps I should have seen the changes in Tribute sooner. His voracious appetite turned weak and uninterested. His playfulness slowed. Where walking him had always required the strength to restrain his enthusiasm and power, he seemed to falter into slow, deliberate steps. At first I thought perhaps he was maturing, learning to slow and pace himself. But even his play with Loni was lackluster. He wandered about the field, sniffing at various patches of grass, almost ignoring Lonesome Dart who stood quizzically, wondering what was wrong with his friend. And then he set his large, limpid brown eyes on me as if to ask: What's wrong with Tribute? Why isn't he playing today?

But Tribute did not play. He lay quietly in the wettest soil he could find and simply remained there until I summoned him to go. Six is not old for a dog, but for a Doberman, sometimes it is ancient. At night, Trib seemed to improve. His appetite resuscitated. Yet he lay somberly on the couch near my feet. The bright enthusiasm of youth that once sparkled in his eyes was now jaded and distant. The animal that picked up his pillow and carried it to the rear door to signal his need to go out was fading. Day to day he refused food but insisted on his walk to the paddock. Each day he grew leaner. Each day it became harder and harder for Loni to rally him to play. In time, Trib lacked the energy to do anything more than distantly gaze at his friend. Before long the morning walks all but exhausted him. Yet if we walked in another direction, Trib stopped, turned and longingly looked for Loni, while the horse nickered and whinnied for his friend.

All this was not without its visits to the vet. Testing, testing and testing again found nothing here, nothing there. "We need to open him up. But if we do and find intestinal cancer, we will put him to sleep immediately." Sudden death. Life and death on the draw of a single card, like gamblers wagering the last dollar on the final hand. And if the cards turn unlucky the game is done, a friend is gone, all hope vanishes on the turn of that one card. So we hesitate, waiting and waiting and waiting to turn that card, to determine whether luck has been unkind.

From time to time, Tribute improved. He ravaged his food because he had not eaten in days. On those days we had hope. Hope that his youth, his former vitality, his strength of will, would carry him through. On those days, we prayed generously and thanked God for having spared our friend. When he lapsed again into his illness and refused his food, we wondered how God could be so cruel as to play such tricks. We cajoled Trib with food to stoke his strength and pumped him with steroids to resuscitate him. Yet, each day he became worse. And each vet visit revealed nothing more than the last. Death can be so indefinite, so agonizingly slow that we hate its impeded progress.

Despite all help, Trib became worse. Each day he became slower, weaker. Each day, the worried glint in Loni's eye deepened. Each visit to the paddock was more traumatic and soul wrenching than the last. Tribute, the long shot dog, was very, very ill and no amount of hope or prayers would save him. He had served whatever purpose was his in the brief time he lived and he would join his sire on the quiet hill where the tall spruce grew and the dark woods beckoned.

Each day, Loni questioned me with large pleading, worried eyes. And for the first time I sensed compassion and love in them. He was begging for his friend, his face taut and frowning. When I peered into his saddened eyes, I knew he was crying. Not from the eyes, but from the soul that is within us all. His friend was dying and we were powerless. He was powerless, bewildered.

I was choked with emotion. Tribute, the long shot dog, was not even supposed to exist. His sire had been at the end of his life and the vet felt he could never impregnate a female after having suffered wobbles and a hernia. Yet I needed Taurus to leave something of himself. So when Nikki conceived and gave birth to five puppies, Tribute alone survived and thus the bond between Trib and Loni was forged in fate because Loni himself had barely survived his birth.

I hated that horse because I deemed him useless and ponderous and yet I never saw such hurt in an animal's eyes. He was puzzled by Trib's lack of response. Puzzled by watching his friend wither to a fraction of his muscular self. There was no light, no joy left in his friend's eyes. Loni was tormented, the loneliness seeping from his eyes, revealing the hurt and sadness there. He was pleading with me, asking me to help and I was an impotent mentor.

In the final hours, Loni nudged me and rested his head on my shoulders. I saw in his eyes a pain so vast I would not have believed it possible. Yet there it was… the soul of an animal laid bare and pure. He was crying. It was his first brush with death and he little understood it. The doubt, the uncertainty welled up in his eyes and for the very first time, I loved him for loving Tribute.

You're telling me my dog is going to die, aren't you? I asked. But all he did was nuzzle deeper into my shoulder. He was mourning and I was his only consolation. And he was mine.

Tribute was almost too weak to walk and home was too far away. If he could not make it I would lift him and gently carry him home. But he rallied and was able to walk. A tribute to his own courage. It was impossible to think of him, weak and helpless, lying limply in my arms. No struggle, no fight, no vibrant life within him. He would not die just anywhere but on the couch where he had been born. And so he did. The vet arrived and wove his magic with the needle of death and Tribute passed into that oblivion where there is no pain, no want, no suffering.

Always, there is that sadness when something dies. Always, that sense of loss. Loni and I shared a common bond because we mourned together. There is in his soul that knowledge that we are bonded by mutual love, by mutual tears, by the pain of deprivation. He reminds me that it is not the loss of an animal friend that has monumental importance but the time we enjoyed together, no matter how brief.

So the horse I loathed and I have bonded in our mutual love for Tribute. And he heralds my own belief that our friends are merely in transition, on the other side of that shadowy veil we call death. I know. I watch him sometimes, as he frolics in the field, bucking, twisting, kicking, dropping his head and charging some imaginary object. It is as though he plays, still, with an invisible friend. Perhaps he is. At least, I like to think he is… like to think our friend isn't really gone at all. It wouldn't be right, after all, for a horse that cries, to be alone. To be without a friend.

These are my friends,
Bright banners unfurled.

These are my friends,
Of the animal world.

Russ

A God Of All Creatures

Why did she punish me? I was good. When she took my leash, I walked proudly beside her right up to her car. Then I sat calmly looking out the window. I only licked her face once or twice. I had always lived with puppies so it was new seeing the hills and grasslands roll past my window. And when we arrived, she took me into the great yard. It was surrounded by a tall, wooden fence. The house had a long, brown porch with lots of good things to sniff and investigate. I knew I would enjoy racing around the yard and playing on the porch. I was so happy I licked her face again. She didn't seem angry but then she chained me to a dog house on a line so short I could barely reach my food and water.

I ate my food but had to back out of my dog house to relieve myself. I kept barking hoping she would come back but she didn't. I heard her car rumble off and she was gone. How I longed for my puppy friends. Then tree limbs faded against the darkening sky. I was alone for the first time in my life. Something was creeping along the wooden fence. It hissed at me and, in the confusion, I knocked over my water. I huddled in my house, almost afraid to move, barking from time to time to scare things off. The lady never came home. Not that night, nor the next day. I was alone, hungry. I barked until my throat was sore. Some people came and fed me scraps and replenished my water, but it wasn't long before I knocked it over again. It was hot and there was no shade. Soon, there was not a lick of water left. So this was to be my new life? My owner would leave me for days and I'd be alone until neighbors came to feed and water me.

After three weeks some strangers came to see me. They put me into a cage and brought me to a new kennel. There were dogs there so I was happy to have company but my front leg kept bending whenever I stood on it.

I heard the people saying no one would ever adopt me. I didn't understand "adopt" but tried to be friendly and to love them. I was only there a few days when a man and lady came into the kennel. They were getting one of my friends, Sweet Pea. I liked the man. He was so short I could spring up and lick his chin. He had a bearded face with kind but pained eyes, and I wondered if they kept him on a short chain too. Kathy, the kennel owner, talked to them and told them I had bone problems. My leg would bow like rubber. He offered to have his vet examine me so someone might adopt me but he didn't need another dog. The lady with him did not seem happy. She told him that it was a mistake to take another dog so soon after losing another family pet. She had a wetness coming from her eyes when she said this but I did not understand why. The man told her it would only be for a short time, and then they would bring me back to Kathy so someone could give me a loving home. The woman was not listening, and she walked away, the man trailing after her. I heard them talking but did not understand why the lady was so upset. She was telling him that she loved Nikki, and it was too soon after her death to have another dog in her place. The man was very gentle and told her that if Nikki were there to speak with them, she would want them to save another dog just as they had saved her. I didn't understand what a dog was but it seemed to have something to do with me. Finally the woman nodded and the man smiled until I thought his fangs would fall out.

I went home with them, very happy that someone loved me. The lady fed me special foods and walked me every day. But I often tired and rested before we could walk home. When I returned the man rubbed my legs. He said I had spunk. At night we sat on the sofa and I would softly chew on his fingers. He offered me cookie treats, too. One for him, two for me. I ate faster than he did. He'd pet me and tell me I was the ugliest dog he'd ever seen but that I reminded him of himself. Well, I had a flat skull, short cropped ears, and a wrinkled neck but I didn't think either one of us was ugly. I just had a hyena head with a Labrador body.

I was free and happy living there. They gave me good food and even the lady was kind to me. I took special pains to help her with her chores, rounding up the horses and barking at them when they scattered away from her. Sometimes, I would jump up so high I could touch their noses, and they reared and went racing off and the lady always had some loud words to say to me. I think she loved me best when she bent to tie her shoes, and I slunk between her legs, reached up and slurped her face. The man always laughed when I did this until I repeated my affections on him, and then it was always fun to see him hopping around with one shoe on and his other foot bare.

The lady took me for long walks. This wasn't easy for me because my front legs bent like rubber bands every time I put weight on them. They just bowed and flexed and gave me a funny gait so the man said I looked like a charging rhinoceros. Every day the man rubbed my legs with something that smelled very funny and tasted worse. And the lady kept giving me pills wrapped in my favorite cheese. Because I grew up having very little food, I gulped the morsels almost without chewing. I didn't mind what they were doing because it seemed they loved me.

When I became stronger, my legs didn't bend as much. I was able to race along the road as the man drove his tractor. And I enjoyed overtaking him just when he thought I was too far behind to catch up. Soon, the lady tramped through the fields with me at her side. She said it was her daily constitutional, and the exercise was good for me. Sweet Pea, their other dog, came along too. The man did not like to walk but he worked on the hills cutting wood and clearing trails. I helped, of course. If he laid his gloves down, I picked them up and chewed them a little to keep them soft and then carried them off to the house so he would have them when he needed them. Sometimes I did the same thing with his shoes and boots. He never seemed to appreciate when I helped him this way but he was so kind it didn't matter if he didn't thank me. I understood.

The lady called me Spunky but the man said I talked too much when I yapped and barked for things so he called me Yappi. It didn't really make any difference what he called me since I was always at his side.

I was very happy in my new home. The lady who kept me when I was first born never came back for me, and it worried me that someday she might. Although I tried to please her, she left me alone for a long time and did not spend any time with me. I spent days waiting for her to come home. When she did, she cleaned where I had messed, gave me food and water and then went to bed. The following morning, she left again and I did not see her for a long time. I was so lonely I just kept howling and barking, hoping she would hear me but she never did. I never understood why she didn't love me. She even left me when the storms came; lightning flashed across the night and set me to shivering even though it wasn't cold. Once, the large tree near the center of the yard sizzled when something struck it. The limb crashed down right near my dog house and I cowered inside, trembling and wet and frightened. But that never happened with the man. When the storms came, he let me into his workroom and kept me near. I would bump against his leg and stand by him.

He understood I was afraid and spoke to me with soothing words. I did not understand the words but I knew I was safe with him.

Although the man and I were friends I did not seem to please the lady. She was kind to me, but did not show the affection the man did so I spent most of my time with him after my morning chores were done. I loved when they rode the horses, too, because Sweet Pea and I would go along the trail with them. We'd explore all the scents and sounds of the woodland, sometimes finding a rabbit or a squirrel. Once I found a funny looking cat with a long white stripe down its back that smelled very bad when I shook it in my mouth. The man and lady bathed me again and again and held their noses for a long time. I never grasped why they always fashioned such ugly faces when I brought these things home to them. Humans are onerous and difficult to understand but they also have a compassion not found in the animal world.

I watched the man as he worked. His hair was near white and his beard curled into tiny balls of gray. He was slower than the woman and seemed to tire sooner. In the afternoon he would disappear for a long time. He always said he was taking a nap. When he returned, I greeted him enthusiastically by jumping up and dancing around his legs. Then I helped him put on his work shoes.

Together we'd go off to work. Many times he'd stop his work to pet me and talk to me. Somehow though, his eyes grew dimmer with each passing day. He seemed to take his nap earlier and earlier. One afternoon he was clearing some brush. I was helping by tugging the branches as he lifted them.

"I don't know why I'm feeling so tired today," he said. "Don't get old, Yap. Stay young. It's terrible when you get old and can't do what you used to. I wish I could run like you, boy. Good to be young again." He bent and massaged my neck.

Suddenly, he just seemed to scrunch down to his knees and laid down for his nap right there in the field. So I lay down next to him but he did not move. It started to rain and still he did not move. It was getting dark. Still he did not move. I was becoming impatient, but it was my task to guard him so I just lay there, waiting for him to awaken. He never did. Then the lady came and other people too. A large white truck came and men carried him into it. I tried to go too but they shoved me out and hurried away. I chased it all the way to the creek and out into the road but the truck moved so swiftly, I couldn't keep pace. It was making loud whining noises which came from the flashing beams on top. I raced so fast I thought my heart would explode and then, the truck disappeared around a curve. I could hear it puffing up the steep hill. Exhausted, I returned to the house, lay down and waited.

A long time later the lady came home. The man was not with her. Other people came and spoke with her. She must have been cold because she was shaking and wet lines were streaking down her face. She ignored me and Sweet Pea but let us stay in the garage.

The man did not come home the next day either. Or the day after that. One day, a long, black car came to take the lady away. She was all dressed in black when I saw her. I had never seen her wear such clothing. Someone came in a car and took her away. She did not smile at us. Not at all. I think she looked like I must have looked when the first lady did not come home to feed and pet me. And then it was just me and Sweet Pea sitting there, waiting. I kept waiting for the man but he didn't come. I missed him. He always talked to me as if I were a human and not an animal at all. He always called me his baby rhino, and his voice was loving and calm. But he did not return.

The lady went away again and, when she returned, Sweet Pea and I knew something was very wrong. Strangers came to care for and feed the horses and leave food and water for us. There were strange sounds coming from the house and at night it was dark and soundless. Next day, a car motored up the driveway. I was happy then because it was Kathy, and I remembered her because she kept many of my friends at her boarding place. She was not smiling. She and the lady spoke for a long time. I knew they were talking about me because the lady nervously glanced at me from time to time but she would not look into my eyes.

I heard Kathy saying that no one would adopt me because of my breeding. I didn't understand that. I just loved people and wanted them to love me. When I barked I was talking, not threatening them, and I loved to play so what did my breeding have to do with anything? Kathy opened the car door and called me. I was so excited. I was going for a ride. I kept waiting for Sweet Pea to come but she was not invited. I barked and kept looking at her as we drove down the road. Why wasn't she coming too? But then, I thought, we were just going for a ride and would come right back.

When we arrived at Kathy's, I understood for the first time I was staying with Kathy. I missed my friend very much and wanted him to come and get me. But Kathy put me in my old cage. I felt sad and disillusioned. I wanted to go home.

If I had to stay with someone, I was happy it was Kathy. She was always kind to me. I guessed it would be all right. Maybe the man would come back and take me home again when he woke up. So I contented myself to stay with Kathy. But she did not keep me either. She took me in the car again. I was so excited that I barked and barked because I was going home. When she drove up to a strange building I had never seen before, I knew I wasn't going home and I wasn't living with Kathy any more, either.

I didn't like the place. It was cold and didn't smell nice. They put me into an end cubicle in a long row of cages filled with other dogs. I was lonely for the man and longed for the days when I trotted beside him in the fields. I wondered what would happen to me. Why was I here?

People came and looked at us. They strolled down the long corridor, peering at each animal, making strange sounds. I always barked and tried to be noticed but no one ever came to pet or even talk to me. Once a little boy made a funny face and said I was the ugliest dog he'd ever seen. I barked and smiled at him and stood up on the gate but he passed right by. Sometimes people came and took a dog out of the cage. But no one came for me. I grew depressed, wondering what happened to my friend and why he was not coming for me. Would I ever find a home and people to love me?

Each day, I looked down the row, and there were more empty cages. The animals never returned. Each day the empty cages drew nearer. Fewer animals. Where had they all gone? Finally a lady in a white smock came. She spoke softly and petted me but I was shaking even though I tried to be calm. I was lifted onto a table and strapped down. Metal clinked as she fastened the straps. But I could see very little. Then the lady approached me with a long needle. She was speaking calmly but her eyes were cold and distant. I wanted to struggle free but I trusted her so I stayed still.

Then a soft voice spoke to the lady in the white dress. It was the lady from the farm. I barked happily and she looked at me.

For the first time she gazed right into my eyes and I saw something I had never seen there before.

"Please," she said, and her voice trembled weakly. "He was my husband's dog. Russ passed away two weeks ago. I know he loved Spunky. He said he would just get him well again and then bring him back for adoption. He'd never do that. I knew that. 'Mr. Softie' couldn't hurt anything and he'd never have brought him back. He always seemed so happy with Spunky. Russ had a very difficult life and was very abused by the people he loved most. I think he saw the same thing in Spunky and bonded with him. Seldom laughed, though. And yet only a while ago, Spunky raced down the front lawn, stopped so abruptly that he skidded and rolled half way down the yard. Russ laughed from deep, deep within his soul and his eyes were bright with mirth. I'd not heard him laugh that way in years. I guess it felt good to hear that. I know he'd want Spunky to have a home. And in a way, Spunky is all I really have of him, so something of Russ survives. He's really part of my husband and I'm not willing to let that go just yet. When I am, Spunky will still have a home with me." She waited and then talked again.

"I didn't think I could keep him. He'd remind me too much of Russ. But now I know it would be a mistake to take him away from the horses and the farm. It would be a mistake for me to let him go. So if you don't mind, I'd like my dog back."

The lady in the white smock nodded. She put down the needle and loosened the strap. There must be something wrong with human eyes because she had wet streaks coming from hers. So did the lady from the farm.

That was two years ago. I am grown now and my legs are fine. They say for a Pit Bull/Shar Pei mix I am not a bad looking dog. The lady does not call me ugly any more. Even the U.P.S. driver says I am a fine looking dog. I always jump in his truck to check his packages and get a pat on the head. The Fed Ex man brings me biscuits too. I always bark when he drives up.

In the morning I go with the lady as she feeds the horses. I don't help as much as I used to, and it's been a long time since I stole any shoes or gloves. I guess I'm growing up. Life is really good here. I have rabbits and birds to chase and bones to chew. When all my chores are done, I rest on the front porch, staring down the long, long road. The lady says my friend is not really gone. He's sleeping just down the road where the woodbine twineth and one day soon we will all be together again. She says it's because love is eternal.

I keep looking down the road but I don't see him. So I wait, patiently wait for my friend to finish his nap. I hope he'll wake up soon. It's empty here without him, and he needs me to make him laugh.

The Long Shot Dog

Tribute was ill. Seriously ill. The bright, yellow fluid on the floor before him, the drooping head and dull eyes wiped even the faintest hope away. He ambled over to his dog food where only days ago he voraciously fed. Nosed it. Turned away. There was never anything half hearted about Tribute. He was the long shot dog with the penchant for life. Sired by Taurus, my ten year old Dobe and the only one of five pups to survive. In his exuberance for life he often dragged me around the vet's parking lot. Yet as I mourned the obvious distress he suffered, I regretted the times I avoided walking him or letting him free.

Trib was bouncy, buoyant and amazingly powerful. No matter how he tugged and pulled, often dragging me through the briars or into the shallow farm creeks, I could not help but admire his strong, sleek lines, the silken, black coat, the long typical snout of the Doberman. He was muscled in front, tapered toward the rear, curved well along the abdomen and held that regal air of royalty. I loved him best when he lay in the rear yard as if he were a great, male lion surveying his domain. But he had other moments too. Like signaling his need to go out by picking up a throw pillow and lofting it around in his mouth until I got the message.

But he was anything but regal now. He was listless, dull. His coat darkened and turned ominously coarse and ragged. His eyes spoke nothing but misery. Day after day, he disgustedly turned away from his food as if he knew he must eat but had no appetite for it.

Six years old. How had the time passed? He was a rollicking little pup, annoying his father and racing under the couch when Taurus took after him. I even recall the day he realized in a panic he was too large to fit under the couch and suddenly had no respite from his angry sire. I said he was the long shot dog and he was. His sire was failing as I was failing. Not from death but from the death of wonder to which all men are subject. Taurus was dying from old age and from cancer; I was dying from retirement and loss of purpose.

Once I knew Taurus's days were near an end and I could not part with him, I purchased Nikki and bred them. The vet said it was a long shot. Perhaps it was, but it was something I willed, because my own survival depended upon it. Thus, Nikki conceived, not by natural means but by that sheer force of will that dictates what must be. She bore him five pups. One by one, they lapsed into death. No reasons known or given. Death claimed the four and left me to bury them and to explain to Nikki why I had taken them. But Tribute survived. And in him, I survived.

He was but a shadow now. I walked him because he had no strength to pull or tug or race away. Now he was the calm, sedate animal I had always wanted, yet I hoped his strength would return. I prayed. I implored God to allow more time. So many days went by with hardly notice paid to my friend. So many nights when an hour more with him would have troubled no one. But I neglected him and took him for granted and now that he was dying, the lost hours gnawed at me. Days came and went as if he had forever, as if I had forever. And the passage of that time was not unlike the passage of our own lives when only a few grains of sand remain in the hourglass of our existence.

Hours before we called our vet, Chuck Keiser, Tribute seemed restless. He wanted to go onto our enclosed porch where he had spent so many years before we fenced the rear yard. He was failing. I could see that. So I had not taxed him with further walks. I watched him as he walked to the end of the porch and looked longingly at the fields beyond.

He did not often run free except to play with his equine friend, Lonesome Dart. I could not control him at liberty and therefore most of his life I restrained him with a leash. Only twice did he break free, once to race up and down the hill behind our house that now bears his name. The other, when he raced to the end of our property and properly dispatched a trespasser. I always thought him a simpleton, too brainless to be worth very much and yet, in those moments of glory every dog inevitably has, Tribute was both noble and courageous. He dispatched the trespasser and proudly returned home to boast of his achievement. But that was yesterday and today, he was failing. No longer could I dominate him. I could only accede to his requests. So I watched him, studied his moods, his moves. Asked him a hundred questions. I caught him more than once staring out the living room window toward the fields where he had played. I fretted because I did not comprehend what he wanted or what was right for him. So I asked.

"What? What do you want, Trib?"

He glanced at me, hardly able to hold himself erect, looked longingly again at the fields. He wanted to walk. It would be his last. It would exert him and hasten his death, but he looked so wistfully at the fields that I couldn't deny his request. When Virginia got his leash, he perked to life. I knew then, it was he who was directing me, for his thoughts were my thoughts and his will, my will.

We walked along the road we always walked. In a while he would walk a road unknown to both of us. His steps were faltering and slow as he lumbered along. And I spoke to him as we hiked. Gone now was the spirit that had pulled and yanked me off my feet so many times. Gone was the bouncy puppy that had never quite grown up. Gone was the dog that licked and slurped my face with love and endearment. Gone was the dog that stole my shoes and hid them in his bed. Gone was he who patiently waited at breakfast so he could lick the last crumbs off my plate. Gone was the friend that lay quietly beside me on our evening couch. Gone was the light in his eyes, only the dull look of Death remained. Coming to an end, too, was our time together.

I told him how much I loved him, how hard I had prayed. How I could not understand why or how this had happened. If he wanted to be free I was prepared to let him go, although he would always remain in my heart. I cried too. Softly. And told him I was sorry for all the hours we had not spent together. He did not look up, he just paced along, carried by the strength that had always sustained him, now stopping to sniff a familiar scent, then moving again.

We reached the little creek by the storage shed and there he stopped. He walked into the water which was shallow from the long drought, but did not drink. Instead, he watched the water slipping quietly on its long journey downstream. Perhaps he was thinking of the journey he was soon to make. Back and forth he trod, stopping to study the creek's silver glow as if pondering the meaning of some infinite message. Still he did not drink. He walked as far as he could and then retraced his steps. When he buckled and nearly fell, I knew it was time to return. I could not help but cry seeing this noble and magnificent animal as death overtook him. We are all helpless before Death. But can we face it as nobly as my companion?

We turned for home, the last walk. And it was then I noted that all the horses were poised by the fences, watching Trib. I walked him near his friends so he could say his good-byes. I dared not think of anything but the moment. His Standardbred friend, Loni, looked down at him with such pity and compassion in his eyes, he surely must have known it was the last time he would see him. In that look, I knew it was true that animals know when death is near. And in that look, I saw the death of my friend, my companion, and I knew this was the last time I would ever walk with him.

His walk was now less sure. He hesitated and gasped for air until I was no longer certain he would make it home. I heard myself calling to Virginia to bring the car, though I did not know how we would get him into it. I resolved to carry him if need be if I could do so without bringing him pain. But he rallied and continued walking, his breathing labored, his steps becoming feebler all the time. To see this magnificent, spirited animal now disintegrating before my eyes filled me with rage against the death which was overtaking him.

We neared the driveway home. Instead of turning up the drive he wanted to go on, but I checked him with the leash. He halted there, still staring into the distant fields, still wondering what was happening to him. When I called him to head home, he simply stared at me quizzically, reminding me we had always walked along the field's edge.

"No,Trib, not this time. Time to go home… time to die. Oh God, why do you take my friend? I know you are with me but there is such pain in seeing him die. No Trib, no more walks. No more play. Why did I not spend more time with you? Why was I not strong enough to train you, to walk you, to tame your wild spirit? Time to go home. You'll die on the couch where you were born. So rest until the doctor comes. There will be others to guide you to this new place and there will be no pain, no hunger, no suffering. The wind and the sun will always be sweet as they were in the fields of home, but now, it is time to go there. I have to let you go."

In truth, I have never let him go.

He labored up the slope to the rear porch where he had bounced so many times, played with his leash at the sheer excitement of going for a walk. But he feared the steps to the front deck. It was the place where once a tiny tree frog had frightened him nearly to death. He hid behind Virginia until the frog was gone. He was lively then, even if afraid. But now there was only the slow, tremulous cadence of a weakening animal, ready to die.

I removed his collar. He walked to the foot of the third floor steps. They must have looked a hundred miles long and he turned away. But I urged him on and told him we would help. We became his feet, his muscle, his sinew, his will, step by laborious step. And when he was four steps shy, he lurched forward and made the landing, entered my study and struggled onto the couch. He lay down, breathing hard from exertion, his nose thrust into the very corner where I had cuddled him as a puppy. When he lacked the breath and had to rise, I supported him, smoothed his face and head, and nibbled his head and ears—something he always liked. But I could see the glaze creeping over his eyes. He was not conscious of much. The vet would come soon, I told him. The suffering would be over then. I wanted the vet to come. To come and help my dog to die. All the words I said fail me now, but I know I said them. "Now I lay him down to sleep. I pray the Lord his soul to keep." More tears, then: "Lord please send Death to take my dog and end his pain."

And all the times I chose my work instead of play, instead of time with him, rushed forward to haunt me. There was no more time. No time remaining for play. No more moments of love, or sitting quietly on the sofa. No time for laughter as he carried the large pillow in his mouth and paraded around the room. The clown was no longer humorous because the clown was dying.

I called an animal psychic. We do desperate things when hurting. But she spoke to animals. She told me that Tribute understood he was dying, that he knew his body was failing and he was disgusted with it. She was right. Trib thought as I did. No use for a body that was pained and failing. He was ready for the next world. So he was not afraid to die. The psychic told me Trib loved me. He did not begrudge me the time I had not spent with him but relished the time we shared. Because he was my friend, I clung to him. Because he was my friend, I put him to sleep.

He knew when the vet came. He did not resist. If there is a world where our friends go, he knew he was going there. He turned only once to look, that contented look in the failing eyes, aware of what was happening and content that it should be so. I told him I would always love him, that the emptiness for me would never tarnish. But he was in the throes of death and paid me no mind.

I stroked his head and soothed him when he hyperventilated until the drugs took effect. He went quietly into that dark night, never resisting, never raging. All the puppy light that had always been in his eyes, withered and dulled. In moments, he was gone. In moments, I was gone too, left with an emptiness that would always plague my soul. I stroked the long, full body so silky smooth and still and hugged him as my heart quickly went out of me. I died as quietly as he had. The vet—my human friend—grabbed my shoulder and squeezed. There were tears in his eyes as well. Trib lay by the small pillow with a Doberman print. His security blanket, I called it. Now, it lay as lifeless as he.

We buried him near the blue spruce where lays his father. The full moon bore witness through bare and lifeless tree tops. It was a still night, starry and windless. The Little Dipper was clear and sharp. We laid him in a Mexican blanket and wrapped him softly in its folds, then lowered him into the grave. On top of him, we set his pink blanket, chewed full of holes where he had shaken it to bits but his bed nonetheless, because it still bore our scent. And finally the two chew toys he loved best, because to see them again would only bring more pain and heartbreak to us and perhaps he would need something in the after- world with which to play. I nudged the soft warm soil over my friend and secured the grave so nothing would violate it. My friend, who understood me so well, whose love was simple, noble and compassionate, lay there wrapped in the blanket upon which he had been born, upon which he had slept. Inside me, lay the hope he would suddenly spring forth and exclaim, "I was only jesting. I'm not dead at all."

I console myself recalling that we had quality time in that last week and a half, that we walked the fields and dreamed the dreams, that we scented the life that lived there and marked the places along the way where hope renewed itself. Here was the place where he drank water, kept it down and trotted at his old pace. Here was the place where he bounded up the slope and here, where he nearly pulled me down. I console myself with the memory of our final walk. On reflection I know that he was preparing me for his death, making certain I would survive, easing me into the pain of loss. Those final days will fade into a mist where pain is no longer reality but oblivion. Tribute will always be in that special place in the heart where all sacred things are laid to rest.

Tribute died that so that I might learn a lesson. Treat every day as if it will be the last we spend with our pet. Take time each day to enjoy the friendship. Let the world slip by unnoticed and be with loved ones, be it animal or human. So he died, not without purpose but that I might learn.

That we are powerless to help those we love pains me not a little. Worse that I did not understand his love, until he was dying, pains me more. And then I understood all too well, that I had been loved in a manner that will never again come in my lifetime. Thus it is not the loss of a dog that pains me but the loss of infinite love which only once in a lifetime approaches the infinite love of God.

I pass the places where we visited, hoping to catch some small glimpse of him. But there is none. Just a presence that seems to say; "I am here. I am waiting."

And as I walk, the place is full of spirits of moments spent, of children and animals at play, of love and loyalty, of moments of hope and desperation, of prayers unanswered. I know now that love is not measured in hours spent together but in the warmth of each other's comfort. It is not the loss which survives, but the love between animal and man. Tribute was my gift from God. His animal soul and I were intertwined. I rejoice in calling him my friend. I give thanks for having had him. My heart is devastated. The spirit of my dead friend lies among the ruins. My own forlorn spirit lies there as well, as I await the time when we are joined again.

How much I mourn
Those who pass,
Who lay before me
In this field of grass.

Their spirits roam
Where my heart can hear
The echoes of their love,
Still near.

Russ

The Talking Horse

He nickered warmly but there was a knowing sadness in his eyes.

Behind him lay the long blue/green strands of Kentucky fescue carpeting the paddock that had for so long been his home.

"We've come a long way in ten years," he projected his voice. "And now, you are selling me."

"It's not an easy decision. Parting with someone after ten years," I replied, looking into the cheerless, brown eyes that had deceived me so many times. "But if anyone deserves it, Willie, it's you. I just got tired of your shenanigans."

"I thought we had a bond between us," he worked his mouth.

"A bond? Yes! I know. I love you. I even think in your own stubborn way, you love me. Yes, we are bonded, when you want us to be bonded and when you don't, well, Willie, you just do as you damn well please."

"I'm a Morgan. Morgans are very proud. But selling me? I just can't believe it."

I gazed at him somewhat sadly. Those soft, deceptive eyes. Those lying eyes that invited me to ride then dumped me at the first opportunity. He had belonged to people in Tennessee; a little girl rode him in 4-H shows and mock fox hunts where he remained undistinguished. She tired of his games and decided on an Arabian instead. So Willie, Sweet William, as they called him, was for sale. I rode him. I bought him. Not because I was ready for another horse but because my first selection, a green trail horse, reared, dumped me, then fell on me, breaking my ribs and my hip. Breaking my spirit. I bought Willie to partner up with my wife who loved horses and trail riding. I bought him to capture the dream of the West where every little boy sees himself a Cowboy Hero.

But Willie was anything but Champ or Trigger. He stood 14.3 hands broadly conformed, with muscular shoulders and a vast hay belly. And he had a disposition to match, brooding, somber, but completely captivating when he wanted something. In my first altercation with him, he did the Willie stomp, a slight rearing off the ground, coupled with a quick thrust of his hip. He learned a simple twist of the hindquarters drove me out of the saddle. He had my number after that. Not that I didn't try. I rode him into the woods, along the fields, and always, it was the same. He went as far as his tiny courage permitted, then seized the bit, spun about like a reining horse and trotted back to the barn. And what a jarring trot it was.

There were times when he was perfectly fine and others when he deliberately sidestepped into brambles, knowing full well I'd catch my arm or leg on the thorns. And he always wore that innocent smirk that hints it was done deliberately. But where is the proof?

He nickered again, waiting for answers.

"Let's review the facts and if you can convince me otherwise, I'll change my mind. How about all the times you carried me under an overhanging branch? You'd head right down the center of the trail, side step into the tree, knock my hat off and then step on it. You did that deliberately."

"I called that cultural renovation. Reshaping your hat was simply in keeping with your personality and your riding ability."

"See what I mean? There's that persnickety, arrogant attitude of yours. That was a $240 Stetson and you call it cultural renovation?"

"I do."

"How about the time you just wandered off and left me standing there with a stack of logs?"

"You were using me as a pack horse, toting logs from the back trail. I resented that. After all, I do have royal blood."

"Yeah, I know. Your great, great grand dam won the Vermont 100 Mile three years in a row, and with a foal to boot."

"Well," his eyes smirked, a point scored.

"Well, on your best day you couldn't walk the trails without stumbling all over the place. Half the time it was deliberate. And you wouldn't leave the barn without another horse, ha! But when Virginia rode you, well, Mr. Handsome was just fine. Carried her all over the place. Not a problem in sight. No grazing on leaves, no stumbling, no refusals, no bucking. What about that?"

"You slouch. You slouch when riding. It throws my balance off and keeps my head down. Of course I stumble. And Virginia's not afraid. She's a real Alpha. She sits a horse correctly, uses her legs for pressure. God, Russell, you're all over the place. You use the right leg when you should use the left, the left when you should use the right and you don't know a flying lead change from a dancing trot. Of course I was better with her. She's a rider. You're a tourist."

"So now you are giving riding lessons?"

"Who better than moi? Face it, Russell. You're afraid and you make me afraid. You're tense, so I'm tense."

"And do I tense when you see a cow, chicken, duck, or deer? Is that why you stiffen and head back to the barn, oblivious I am even in the saddle? You name it and cautious Willie runs from it."

"The ad said sensible."

"What ad?"

"The ad you read when you were looking for a horse. It said "sensible". Besides, those cows came out of the woods. How was I to know what they were? And they smelled bad."

"That's not the half of it. All those times you bucked me off just because I asked you to do something you didn't want to do. You've got a temper, Willie, and an attitude problem."

"You didn't think so that night at East Fork when you found yourself seven miles from camp and darkness all around and no flashlight. Then you asked me to get you home before it was pitch dark. Do I get credit for that?"

"You've been living off that credit for five years. How about our first trail ride? I strolled off into the woods to relieve myself and you panicked because you thought I'd left you. Did I not lead you into the woods with me to ease your fears? I usually do not have company when I pee."

"You did. But what about that time the saddle slipped under my belly with you still in it? Did I run off and bash you along the ground like a bouncing ball?"

"No, score one for you. Come on, I'll groom you."

"I'd rather you just turn me out along the road so I can graze."

"Sure. Like I've done a hundred times before when I felt sorry for you. And when I'd come to fetch you, you'd deliberately run off. What about that? You'd soft-soap me with those pleading eyes and then laugh when I came to get you. Run me all over the damn farm."

"I was expressing my individuality. There are always differences between man and beast. But selling me? That's a low blow."

"Willie, things are bad between us. You've dumped me. You jar my teeth when you trot. All right you've got a nice canter but you won't go more that fifty feet before you stop. Your mind wanders on the trail. You're always looking for something to eat. It's gotten so I wouldn't ride you if my life depended on it."

"You over-tighten the reins. It's the fear factor again. So I buck you off to teach you a lesson. Only you never learned," he argued.

"Then I started you with the beginners. Thought I could trust you. You fell asleep with my daughter riding you and fell flat on your face."

"It was a boring ride. Your daughter has nothing interesting to say."

"Then I trusted you with my pregnant daughter-in-law and you lunged up a half mile hill with her hanging on and screaming. I thought she was going to deliver right there on the trail."

"If it did induce labor I would not have charged you a medical fee." He turned away, the hurt welling in his eyes. I rubbed his muzzle and remembered the good times. Few, but some good times. Willie had his days and I had mine. They just seldom coincided.

He was getting to me and I needed more ammunition. "Then there was that little girl, Tori, who had never ridden before. I trusted you to carry her well and you plain ran off with her. And then there was Samantha who really was taken with you and you galloped her all the way back to the barn, her screaming and whooping all the way. Scared the hell out of both girls and neither one of them ever came back for another ride."

"Young people enjoy excitement. I thought I was making their ride an eventful one. Besides I'm a Morgan, not a bicycle with training wheels."

I moved him into the barn, me walking, him ambling with that shuffling, stumbling gait. Willie always shuffled when he didn't want to go somewhere. I recalled then how sluggish he had been when I bought him. Under saddle he always looked good, like a trail horse should look. I loved to observe the shadow of the two of us as we rode along the roadway. I recalled his lineage, from the Lippet Morgan line, the "do anything, go anywhere breed", and I silently mused that if anything did not apply to Willie, it was the Morgan characteristic. I could not avoid wondering what went wrong.

In point of fact Willie walked where his eyes took him, side to side, looking ahead to the next place to graze, stopping along side the trail to munch ferns, briars or beech leaves. His eyesight was impeccable and he could spot three strands of clover at a hundred yards. Keeping him going in a straight line was a chore in itself and I blamed no one but myself because I alone was at fault for his behavior.

We moved into the shadow of the barn. He led willingly, not halting at all. It was a familiar routine. He stopped where I often groomed and tacked him up and he was as sullen and uncaring as he had always been. Food was his only motivation. Food his only loyalty.

Some animals will work for food. Some will love for food. But Willie loved only the food and gave no loyalty or respect in return. I am angered at how often I'd spoiled him with carrots and apples, thinking some vestige of loyalty might gain me his respect. I wondered how often he sensed a bribe to disguise my unbridled fear. Oh yes, he knew I was afraid. He'd smelled the fear the first time I rode him, sensed the fear the first time he reared and stomped when I prevented him from grazing. He was one horse on the ground and another under saddle. Somehow he knew. And thus when I accidentally spurred him lightly, he galloped away with me, under his own control and halting only when I rolled limply out of the saddle.

No, it was not the last time. Just when it seemed he and I had found that bond, that niche, Willie dumped me again. But it was more. I loved him as a pet but I had failed to control him as a horse. Willie was not a dog or a cat. He needed leadership, the security of the herd, of the alpha. I had hardly been that.

"You're grooming me early. Are they coming today?"

"Who?"

"The people you are selling me to."

"Who told you I was selling you anyway?"

"It's all over the farm. Come on, Russell, Uno told Blaster who told Dusty who told Red. Red passed it on to me two or three days ago."

"What a gossip mill. I always suspected you guys talked between yourselves. It was just too coincidental that my other riding horses tried the same stunts you pulled."

"Ha, of course, blame it on the horse. Just like a human! If you had been alpha, I would have respected you. I needed tough love, not maudlin sentiment." He snickered, then donned that bored look he wore when we tacked up for the trail.

"Well, old buddy, we've come a long way but I've really had it with your attitude."

"I guess," he yawned. "Anything to eat? Carrots? You always have carrots."

"That's your motivation, Willie. Food. I never understood why my kindness was never rewarded."

"You can't bribe a horse. We're above that. I needed to know you'd keep me safe if something came after me."

"It's not supposed to work that way. It's supposed to be a trail ride. But then you started sidestepping into branches and trees. Can't tell you how many knee knocks I got, even with plenty of room between the trees. And how many boots did you tear up, accidentally on purpose stepping on my foot?"

"I like to spread out. I only stepped on a toe anyway, never your whole foot. Never did that. Where's that carrot?"

I spoiled him. I always had. A horse can't be bribed with treats. Not even with love. He needs leadership. As I thought about Willie, I understood that one either controls life… or it controls him.

"Carrot?" he repeated.

"All right," I sighed. "I'll get you one. Lord, I'll get you one. You know it always comes as a reward if you give me no trouble cleaning your hooves. Then another if you don't play games with the bridle."

"I never give you trouble with any of that."

"Oh no? For over a year you kept turning your head. When that didn't work you raised it up because I was too short to reach that high."

"Lord, don't give me that old line again that God punishes horses who take advantage of short people. I'm sick of that one."

"No, it never made any difference, did it? I could talk to Uno and he seemed to understand. Could talk to Red and he'd work with me. But not you, Willie. Willie always goes his own way."

"It's what the market will bear. If you push and the other guy gives, it's not my fault. And by the way wasn't it Red who spooked and tossed you pretty hard when the squirrels scared him? Three broken ribs, a broken collar bone and a punctured lung. You were out of commission for three months on that one. Is that my fault?"

"No, I guess it isn't. It's mine. Not enough rider for you or for him. It's not like that in the Westerns. The horse just always does what his rider wants unless he's scared by a rattlesnake. But there are also horses that are forgiving. Not you Willie."

"If I didn't forgive, you'd have more bruises than you do. And another thing. How about all the times you and Virginia were battling and I had to listen to those complaints? One end of the trail to the other. Whine, whine, whine. If you're so unhappy why don't you sell her?"

"She's not property. You don't sell your wife."

"Only your horse. Huh!"

"We could carry this dialogue all day but we don't have time, Willie."

"So it's true. They're coming to buy me, aren't they?"

I tacked him up and he stood as always, quietly subdued, munching on the carrot bits I palmed for him. It was hard to believe this might be the last time he and I rode together and I didn't know whether to rejoice or cry. It's not easy parting with a friend, even a fickle one like Willie. I'd made mistakes with Willie and they worsened with time. It was too late to begin again. All I could do was to start over with another horse.

I mounted the block and swung into the saddle. He stood as he always stood, unmoving until I gave the signal. Then we plodded up the gravel road in that slow, deliberate gait that meandered sluggishly to the first turn. We had never ridden the trail alone. There came a point when I tensed, expecting the worst. But Willie plugged along as though we had done this every day for years. We turned into Lonesome Trail until it wound down and joined with Outlaw Trail and then onto Swamp Trail, which traversed a mile and a half. He was perfect. Not a single glimmer of fear and then we were at the far end where the trail switched backed on itself. I could have taken the lower trail home but instead I summoned my own courage and turned him to the far fields of a neighboring property.

"Feeling daring, today?" he asked.

"You've never been this good before. What's wrong?"

"Wrong? Nothing wrong with me champ. You're more relaxed than ever before. I can feel when you tense and you're starting to already. When you stress, I stress. See? You're tightening your legs in the stirrups because you expect trouble. What trouble? When you tense I'm out of here and that's when you get dumped for trying to restrain me."

We turned into the field that bordered our property. Across that field and across a creek lay a section of forest we seldom rode. But we rode there that day and Willie was fine. But I knew it couldn't last. We turned homeward at a slow walk. I urged him into a canter which was always his best gait but being the indolent horse he was, he only cantered a few yards and then returned to his walk. I knew that if I urged him again, he'd buck me off and wanting to end it on a happy note, I relented and permitted him to walk homeward to the barn.

I unsaddled him and rubbed him down with alcohol, massaged his legs, cleaned his feet again and groomed him until he glittered like gold sparkling in a sunlit stream. I fed him carrots and ran my hands over his smooth, bay coat and then, in silence, we waited.

The white trailer lumbered up the long, gray road to the barn.

Happy people alighted from the vehicle, a fourteen year old girl with flaxen, fluffy hair, the rough cut father who docily let the women enthuse over Willie and the mother who seemed to know what needed to be known. They rode him. Again and again, up and down the road. My heart rode with them, half worrying Willie would surprise them with his array of antics, half worrying that he wouldn't. It was difficult to believe I was finally ready to let him go. Part of me was not. It was not easy to admit my mistakes, to acknowledge failure. Yet, from failure we build monuments of personal achievement.

The hour before the potential buyers came Willie and I had gone out on the trail. He had handled beautifully as if to thwart my firm convictions to send him away. The severing of a bond is never easy and is less so for a man who lacked his mother's attention---attention his siblings received while he carried the family financially. To him fell the burden of disciplining the younger children. After working endless hours, racing home for five hours sleep and off to college, there was not a note of thanks or gratitude, not a single acknowledgment of his worth.

It was not easy selling Willie, or for me to recognize my failure. I failed with Willie. I had no plan, no direction, no understanding of him as an individual. Because I loved him there was but one gift I could give him. The gift was to sell him to people who could understand him, who could ride him, who could control him, who could give him purpose. I was not that person. All I could do was render him useless. For a fine animal such as Willie, that was a pitiable waste.

I failed with Willie but I also learned what is needed to control a horse. With that knowledge, perhaps I might never again have to part with an animal by sale.

He preened over the attention he received, drew himself to full measure as I had never seen him. He nuzzled the little girl and charmed the mother. He behaved beautifully when the inexperienced father mounted and rode him and piqued me by going further along on the trail than he had ever gone with me. I watched as the culmination of ten years of hope and disappointment circled and side stepped and trotted with the slow, smooth trot he was seldom capable of with me. Oh no, with me, everything had to shake and rattle, jar my teeth, slam my spine in and out of the saddle with pounding thumps. It was never an easy time with Willie.

He returned to the barn, ambled straight up to me and nuzzled my shoulder. This was what he wanted.

"Will you tell Beth you sold me?" he whispered.

"Yes, Willie. I'll write and explain."

"You won't say anything bad?" he frowned.

"No Willie. Just to explain why I let you convince me this was right for you. Besides it was my fault, not yours. Perhaps I'll do better with the next horse."

"Be firm," he whispered, so tenderly I almost cried. Then, he loaded calmly into the trailer, eager to begin his new adventure.

I tried to look away. After all, it was only a horse. He wasn't dying, just moving to a new home. Someone else's home. He looked around at me, saying a last goodbye and then the door slammed shut. The trailer again drove up the patched, gravel road, slowed at the creek and splashed through it. I heard it clanging along the roadway just as a door in my life had just clanged shut. I stood in the disbelief of one who commits to an action and finds no acceptance in the resolution.

The purchase price seemed little consolation. It was not money I needed but absolution from failure. If ever I understood how Judas felt, it was lamenting the money that lay before me.

And then, as I had promised, I turned to the computer and wrote to Willie's former owner, Beth.

Dear Beth,

I am writing because I sold Willie today. I have no excuses but my own failure as a horseman and as a person. It was difficult letting him go after ten years. I had no alternative, either for him, or for me. He was neglected, not in the sense that I did not care for him physically but in the sense that I could not meet his emotional needs. He languished in disuse because I was afraid of him. He idled alone in his paddock because he terrorized the other horses at feeding time.

Day after day I passed by his paddock while he called to me. It pained me to hear that call. It pained me not to ride him. Times when he got to me, I saddled and rode him but my bones always paid the price. It was as if he deliberately lunged up the hills with his roughest gait or intentionally offered his worse trot.

I remember seeing a photo of Willie in his carriage attire. He seemed so smart, so proud. Much happier than trail riding. He always felt it beneath his dignity to carry a rider and worse, having an amateur afraid to let him run full out and exercise him as he needed. I did not have full control, of myself, of him.

So months passed and then a year, then two. Willie called and I'd pet him, groom him and let him out to graze along the roadway where the grass was tall and green but I knew he wasn't happy here. He had no respect for me, no confidence in me and I had no trust in him. I guess he was too much horse for me but I choose to think I was not man enough for him. We needed a showdown I could not give him. He needed a leader I could not be. In the end the only strength I could muster was to hide my failure by selling him.

The people who purchased him fell in love with Willie at first sight. They are good people and he will be better cared for because they are strong enough to handle him. It's funny but the other day I was thinking of the first major trail ride Willie and I made. I had to go off into the woods and relieve myself and Willie kept calling as if he thought I would abandon him. Turned out I had to walk him into the woods with me before I could pass water. Right behind me, Willie was doing the same thing.

He wanted to go. I know that. When I saw his willingness to walk up the loading ramp into the trailer, I knew it was really his decision to go, not mine. I could sense him saying: "Russell, I have to go. I need something more than you can give me. It's the right thing for both of us."

Knowing that makes it easier, but it does not make it easy. I look for him in his paddock. He isn't there. I wait for his call. It doesn't come. But I gave him a gift, the gift of happiness, people who can ride him, truly care for him and a little girl who will shower him with love in a way I never could. Somehow I always felt he never forgot your daughter, never stopped loving her. And I could not take her place. So he has returned again home and he has his little girl to love him. His gifts to me are the memories we shared and the lessons he taught. My gift to Willie was to set him free.

With sadness,

Russell

Willie.
He is gone because I failed.
Failed to be strong when he needed strength.
Failed to be firm when he needed guidance.

It was not Willie who failed, but me.
But from this failure
A new wall builds that learns
And thus, never fails again.

Russ

To Love A Crooked Horse

Some men lose their wives to other men. Still others to children and grandchildren. I lost my wife to a horse. A crooked horse. Perhaps my wife was never really mine at all. Perhaps they just loaned her to me for the young years, the good years. And then, when time had taken its toll and we were no longer young, they took her back. Perhaps that is the cruelest of all fates. Yet, if a man has to lose his wife, better to lose her to a crooked horse that needs the love, the attention, the care. The horse, at least, will show gratitude. Humans will not. Better to cast the seed into the animal that will appreciate it than to squander it on thankless children or hapless adventurers who spirit wives away.

I lost her to a horse named Frenzy, bent and malformed when she came to us, gnarled not by age so much as by years of breeding and re-breeding until all the life went out of her and there was nothing left but distrust and pain. I cannot speak for the horse. Someone else has already done that better than me because I did not know the animal as well. I knew the wife who attended her. I watched her pace the long gravel road to the weathered barn, through fog, rain or cold and sometimes in bright sunlight. I watched her walk through the long field to the favorite trees where Frenzy savored a cool breeze wafting from the creek. She strode with purpose and resolve, for she was a female attending a female. She carried the grain bucket out to Frenzy each morning and twilight. And coaxed her to eat, handful after handful. I watched that beautiful woman showering such love on that crooked animal and I secretly wished that I were crooked too. But old marriages do not a real bond make and, in time, indifference became a sadness between us.

Yet, never between her and the horse. Frenzy was hurting and crooked and her legs were twisted and gnarled. Every few weeks, we propped her up as best we could and helped the farrier trim her feet. It seemed to help the old mare walk better, stand straighter. I saw my wife when she returned from a summer squall, rain sliding down her face and slipping off her thin lips as if someone had tilted a cup and water dribbled out of it. Saw the fretful look on her pale countenance. The worry spilled from her eyes and in the spillage were the questions:

Will she last the winter? Can we get her through her next shoeing? She is losing weight. What else can I feed her? And worse, will I know when it is time? Will Frenzy tell me? Will she simply lie down and die one day or will she leave that decision to me? God, I dread that. How will I know when? What if I act too soon and she is not ready? What if there is hope for a cure? What if I find a magic lamp with three wishes? Ridiculous the torment we endure.

That's what I saw in those fretful eyes; the worry of a woman in love. In love with an animal. In women, there is unity, cohesiveness and loyalty. For what woman will not turn against her own spouse to defend her child? Or is it jealousy that speaks?

Each morning, Virginia rushed to the drapes and tore them back, as if in awakening she sharply recalled some urgent responsibility. Then her eyes settled on the old mare still standing in the field, down by the wooden fence where the shade of the trees and the breeze cooled and comforted her. She was covered with thick hair. Not winter hair that horses shed in summer. Frenzy never did shed out even when Virginia took the shedding blade and removed the hair to cool her. In the end the hair grew back because Cushing's disease made it so. In addition to everything else, Frenzy had a glandular problem. But despite her twisted conformation, the old mare wore a crown of royalty for she carried a tall dignity about her that labeled her as aristocracy. Yes, her hip was twisted around and her leg hung down at an odd angle. When she walked, she defied the laws of gravity. She should have fallen. But royalty does not fall so there was nobility about her as though she were a queen. When Virginia ambled through the rough fields to mete out Frenzy's food, it was as if royalty were serving royalty because in my wife there was also that tinge of blueblood that set her apart from other women, the upbringing that only nobility endows.

They were very much alike. Frenzy was distrustful and cynical although outward appearance cast her as stoic and trusting. In much the same way Virginia was distrustful, cynical, even a little bitter. An auto accident had changed her once kind and loving demeanor to the distrust of one who has been harmed in an indelible way. So I often thought of them as very much alike, the lady in waiting attending her majesty the queen. I thought of Frenzy as she dominated other mares, pushing them aside, exerting authority over them. I recalled my wife's early school years where she, a loner, stood aloof and dominant among her school friends. I thought of the subservient role I had taken in Virginia's life because my own roots were so inferior to hers. And yet, this pinnacle of aristocracy condescended to nurse a dying, twisted animal and love a frightened, insecure man. How warrior- like are women. How boundless their understanding.

Each day Virginia waited until Frenzy entered the shelter and once there, she massaged the aching spine, rubbed the pained legs with liniment and pain blockers. I wondered how she ignored her own pain, the pain of broken ribs, jaw, spine, the pain of a punctured lung and concussion. Yet she ignored her own pain to attend a dying mare. Something in that bond elevated my respect for this woman so changed by a near fatal accident. Something in that bond elevated my respect for the mare so distrustful of people.

Her distrust caused her to sniff and investigate even the treats I offered her. Hers was a story of use and abuse, a breeding machine, without care or love or proper nutrition. And yet, she had paid a handsome dividend, producing money making horses that brought high prices at the sales and earned their keep on the race track. One would have thought her handsomely rewarded, but in the end her reward was to be donated to an experimental program at a national college. When they'd finished poking her, injecting her, trying different supplements on her, fooling her with apples and carrots and treats loaded with their experimental medications, she was then ceded to a retirement foundation —an old age home so to speak, one that could provide only basic care. Technical care. Not because they did not care but because the demands of so many animals in distress permitted only limited attention.

I watched my caring wife gently massage the hurting legs. Stroke the withers with soft hands. I watched her brush the mane and untangle the hundred snarls in the old mare's tail. I watched her wash the dirt gently from her mare's eyes and groom the coarse hair with a brush sweetened with conditioner. As she crooned to the old mare, the horse understood and nickered. I admit I was jealous of the time she spent with Frenzy, yet my admiration for the animal kept me silent.

Although the mare never knew it, it was I who found the remedies that made her life easier. It was I who delved into medical books trying to make her life more comfortable. It was I who supported her when she could not stand and be shod. But it was Virginia who gave patience, understanding and love. So it was unjust one day, when Frenzy threw a tantrum and galloped around the small paddock, that Virginia never saw her antics and never saw her success. But it came. The old mare was angry with me for taking her pasture-mate away and not turning her out to graze. So she kicked like a young filly and bucked her way across the paddock to show her displeasure and in the end she lapped the paddock four times. It was her last fling, for I never saw her do it again. Virginia never saw it at all but it did not lessen her joy when I told her. Life is neither fair or nor just.

When a fly mask irritated Frenzy's eyes and nearly blinded her, Virginia experimented with new masks and treated her eyes with medication. The old mare trusted her and never flinched. I saw something haughty in that mare, something that understood that help. She never blinked. Her courage and trust never wavered. So gently did Virginia bathe the eyes and insert the ointment until Frenzy was whole again. And as I watched I recognized in my wife the capability for great love, a love everyone could share. Was it a love anyone could share? Was it really that simple? Just to accept that the love is there and join?

Each day I watched the old mare drag her tortured body across the open paddock, to station herself under the spreading sycamore that provided shade, and stand in the breeze that whisked up from the creek. She'd worn the ground as smooth as polished dust. I wondered when she would go down that final time. Would it bring my wife back to me although the years had not done so? Would she be again the smiling girl so docile and naïve? She had been all those things once. Once, she had patience beyond patience for I was a trying man. Once, she had been willing to put me before other people, other things. But then, there was that awful bombardment of metal clashing on metal and the world changed and everything else in life seemed more important to her. Perhaps it put aside the pain she felt. I do not know.

I thought she survived the auto accident as Frenzy must have thought she survived the experimentation. But Virginia did not. Nor did I. We perished in that accident as surely as Frenzy's calcium and minerals levels diminished from years of misuse. What remained were two broken, disillusioned people, searching to find each other again.

What remained of Frenzy was a mere fragment of lost youth and happiness. What evolved in Frenzy was suspicion, distrust and indifference. And it was this indifference I saw in Frenzy as if she could mouth the words that said:

"I have been there, seen it all. No one can be trusted. No one cares. Everyone is here to hurt me or bring me pain or use me. Why? Was it my royalty they hated? Was it my success as a broodmare? Was it the arrogance of leadership? Was I merely property to be used and disposed of? What crime did I commit? Was I too proud because I produced strong foals? Was I too vain because they raced and won and earned large purses? Or did they simply not care? Why, then, should I?"

So all I saw in Frenzy was indifference, to me, to the farm, to the pet dogs we befriended, even to herself. And only one person meant anything to her. And to that woman, only one animal meant anything. An insecure animal may acquire trust, trust that grows and swells with love. But an insecure man is seldom anything but an insecure man. Thus, the animal deserved the care and I did not. Perhaps, that is why I was lonely and alone. I chose to be alone. Frenzy did not. She chose to be loved.

Loneliness is sad. I watched that animal depressed by pain and age, stand quietly in the field, moving only steps at a time. She did not want to die. It was the love, the caring that kept her alive. It was the woman who sat next to Frenzy as she lay in the field. This mare, this breeding machine that pumped out weanling after weanling, stood abandoned in her pasture, grazing and waiting for the day she gave birth. Then some attention came, but it was not the same. The care was for her foal and not so much for her. And she raised the foal, nurtured it and cared for it but was never allowed to keep it. She was much like the mother Virginia had been with her own children; she nurtured them and cared for them, though they did not love her nearly as much as I loved her or even as much as Frenzy loved her. Much as the children I had loved whose memory of me has faded. But not

Frenzy. Every kindness mounted and accumulated until even I was honored with her trust.

One could see the pain in the mare's eyes. She was in foal twenty-three of twenty-six years. The constant weight- bearing drained her bones of needed calcium, making her twisted anatomy gnarl even more. Frenzy learned to run from men, to evade them in the pastures. Men did her no good, only subjected her to more discomfort.

As time inched by, her condition worsened. She became as stiff legged as when she first clamored off the trailer that brought her to us, so shaky we thought she would fall on us. But stalwart and ever the image of royalty, she stood her ground, defiant, noble and free. It became more difficult to shoe her. Three of us had to support that great weight and lift her so the farrier could balance her feet and finally then, she could only be shod when lying in the field. The surprise of seeing the farrier lying next to my wife as he angled the feet correctly still rings with me. But it was necessary. After all, my wife was only on loan to me. Or so I thought. I had borrowed her from her children, from my children. I made her mine. But she was not mine. One day I had to return her for she belonged to others. Frenzy had come along and now Virginia belonged to her as well.

It was no easier to know that than it was for Frenzy to know she was merely a conduit to material wealth; that when her days were finished and her health depleted to the point of no return, she would be abandoned and discarded. It was an uneasy thought for all of us.

Each day we studied her eyes. Was there a sign she had given up? Was she ready for death? Some animal organizations, so called animal lovers, make great sport of happily sending their animals into death to reduce their numbers. Some believe that other dogs come to carry away a dying dog. Swing low, sweet chariot. I do not know if that is true, although sometimes I feel the spirits of all my lost animal friends still haunting me. What I do know is that death is forever; its invitation should not be taken lightly.

We watched her drag herself across the pasture. We watched her valiantly meet each day with that indomitable strength with which she met her life. She'd lie in the warm sun, rise with difficulty, then spin until her hind end caught up with her fore legs.

Steady now, Frenzy, no panic. Just stand easy and you're up big girl.

Each attempt took more effort, brought her nearer to the edge.

The vet was able to do little except tell us that she was not ready to die. Too much brightness in her eyes. Too much determination to enter into death. She'd probably tell us when it was time. But she never did.

There is too much spunk in those who fight for life to ever whisper, "I surrender."

My wife worried that winter would find Frenzy unable to rise. But winter passed and the old mare still rose and peaked like the cresting waves of an eternal sea. Rise and fall. Fall and rise. Eternal. On into summer, with her long hair still growing and the shedding blade and the cool breeze down by the creek to cool her. My wife took to blanching her with alcohol to cool her skin, for she came less and less into the shelter. I watched her limping across the jagged field to spend the night within. Sometimes it seemed she moved hardly at all. The day passed and she remained near the very same spot as the day before. My wife worried about her as she worried for me through my cancer, through my chemotherapy and she did so because she was royalty with dignity and spirit of nobility. I survived. So did Frenzy. I venture Frenzy was my wife's only consolation in that dark period of life. So she remained silent and gave no sign to Virginia that she was ready to die. After all she was needed. As never before in her life, Frenzy was needed.

She weathered yet another winter and stayed the course as I returned to health. During that time my wife was her friend. And she was friend to my wife. When I saw her again she seemed no different than before and yet she struggled to keep her feet and her eyes seemed more forlorn than I remembered. I silently wished I could give her my strength, my years of life. I had no use for them as she did. But life is seldom ours to give.

Frenzy had been down for three days. It hardly seemed any time at all, but she had been down for three days, refused her feed and simply lay there. We were not sure if she rose at night so each evening Virginia traipsed out and stayed by her side, while I waited for dawn to know the outcome of that long night. Virginia's heart was at an end. She had cared for her friend for many years but now she was lost for direction. I did the unpardonable. I shouted and cursed at the old mare and whipped her rump with a towel, snapping it to make more noise. I literally drove her to her feet and willed her to stand. She rose because dignity compelled it, but she went down again and lay exhausted. I apologized to her amid my own tears and she signaled her forgiveness with her eyes. The old mare that had walked away from me, who had run me around the pastures, who refused to trust me, understood and absolved me from my sin.

And then there were two of us crying, my wife and myself, and I no longer begrudged the old mare the time she had taken. I no longer begrudged her life. I willed her to rise. I willed her to live. But in the face of death my will was insignificant. The vet rushed to our farm. It was plainly a call he never wished to make. We tried once more to get her to her feet, but she could not hold her balance. Then the vet performed his task

Now the great mare was dead. She lay still upon the warm ground.

The wife I thought I'd lost turned and fell into my arms. She was warm and soft. Her tears slipped down her face and fell onto my shoulder. That once strong woman was clinging to me for need. I held her near. Spoke words to soothe her aching heart. In her time of hurt and misery, my wife returned to me.

It was then I understood. The love she bore for Frenzy was born of the love she felt for me. Frenzy had merely been a caretaker until I could understand the love my wife had for me. Frenzy had known this for she was wise. And now, I knew it too. That no one who loves an animal as intensely as my wife loved Frenzy can do so unless they have first loved a human.

Frenzy lies now by the copse of trees where she spent so much of her time, where the cool breeze can comfort her and the warm sun can ease her pain. I believe she came to us to teach the lesson of love, of enduring faith. She came to teach the lesson of hope and courage for it takes both to face life on a daily basis.

She lays now in the sight of those who loved her and who forever keep her alive in the memory of their hearts. She shared my wife with me when both horse and man had need of her. Once I had learned the value of life and possessed the courage to face it, she left us to find a better world. May she always rest in green pastures and be free from fear and pain.

I passed by her grave the other day
while mowing the field in which she lays.
I came to the place where she is buried.
She stands there still, tall, straight
and not crooked at all.
Death has given her a dignity
she never enjoyed in life.

Russ

The Cardinal

This could be a story about Nikki's life, but it is not. It is a story of something which occurred after her death. It is also a story about a man I met at the hospital. The man I met stared back at me from a looking glass in one of those dismal rooms they call a hospital toilet. This man was graying, unkempt and uncombed, perhaps sixty-five or seventy years of age. His face was callow and livid white. His cheeks were sunken and wrinkled. The eyes that were once bright with wonder were dull and pitiful. He looked old, terribly old. From his nose a tube ran down into a plastic bag. There were other tubes leading in multiple directions so that he was limited in his movement and unable to see more of this man staring back at him. But he had no desire to see any more of him for the man looked lifeless and wan, as if he should have died, yet somehow lived. Perhaps he was dead already and just didn't know it.

Time upon time, nurses entered his room, thrusting needles into his arm or rolling him about to wash and clothe him with the long, clinical gowns which come undone in the back so that one's rear anatomy is there for public view. Gowns that are done with strings that tie behind where no one can reach and thus to have some modicum of modesty, one must ask total strangers to fasten the back. Even nurses then are strangers as is every new face which appears.

As I stared into this man's face, I saw a stranger. He wore my body, and he held my thoughts but he was not me. I asked him who he was. He replied that he did not know. I asked him if he were alive or dead. He did not know that either. He knew only that he had come to this hospital for routine testing and was whisked into emergency surgery as quickly as he undressed. He only knew that whatever they inserted into the intravenous tube in his arm made him feel wonderfully comfortable and drowsy. He recalled awakening on the operating table and being frigid. Some unseen weight crushed him into the operating table and he labored to breathe. Finally, in desperation, he knew he was about to die and thus, he relented and resigned himself to death.

He must have died and this stranger assumed my body because he did not look like any man I had ever seen. And yet this stranger knew that on that morning, his Doberman had died and his time for delaying surgery had run out. Virginia and I both knew Nikki was dying. She had suffered seizure after seizure. Her love had willed her to remain with us for as long as we needed her. The need having merged with my own need for surgery, we could no longer care for her and she died. The power of love is often so staggering that we live for the possession of it, and we die for the lack of it. The coward may die many deaths but so does the person who thinks himself unloved. Inwardly I knew that Nikki was dead but what did it matter for I was facing death too.

I stared at her lying on the floor before me, hardly able to conceive a life without Nikki. Her six year old son had predeceased her by three months and now, at the moment when doubt clouded my own continued existence, there lay Nikki. We did not have any time to bury her because my time was assigned. I had ignored intestinal problems I knew to be cancer and destiny decreed that Nikki die on that very same day of my hospitalization. So Nikki lay unburied on the front porch and I went forward to meet another fate.

They slit my gullet down the middle of my navel, cut out the tumor and a skilled surgeon took my innards in his hands and searched for cancer. When he was done, he replaced everything and stitched the colon together minus the affected part. What they could not stitch together was my will to live. I viewed life as one massive rejection and thrived on the pain. So much of what we are lies in the past. My father had little time for me. When he did, he filled the hours with the wisdom and advice that would cripple me for years to come.

"Just when you want life the most, son, you die." Or. "Never let a woman know you love her or she'll tear your heart out."

I saw him angered and raging because my mother goaded him to anger. This peaceful, loving man whose family was a deep part of him had been gradually squeezed off until he could not visit his own mother just two doors away. And, as a child, ill with bronchitis and allergies, alone in the dark on the third floor of our home, I waited an eternity as I screamed for her. Nights when the pneumonia choked off my air and left me breathless and terrorized, mom was busy on the phone checking on daddy or consulting fortune tellers. The same rejection I felt from dad, I felt from a mother who had little desire to raise a child, a mother for whom no achievement was ever good enough.

"Yes, you got an A, but you could do that all the time." Or to my suggestions on how to earn money: "You think it's that easy to make money? Are you cracked?" Or if I recited a grade school poem for someone: "Oh, he did it better yesterday."

No friend was ever worthy enough. My social growth with girls was her prime target. Mother drove off female after female by clandestine conversations with their parents until I thought myself misfit and worthless, unable to hold a woman. In the end mom rejected me totally, refusing to call, refusing to acknowledge me. She lived within a very small box. In that box she kept a husband and a son. It was not permitted to tread beyond the perimeters of that box. It was not encouraged to savor life or experiment with reality. Mom willed and her world obeyed because it was contained in this tiny square of anger, regret, disillusionment, fear and guilt. I thought I escaped the box by marrying. I was wrong. The box became smaller because it now contained my first wife who felt very comfortable in such a contained space. Do not let the mind dare to hope or to think or to experiment. My mother never forgave me for venturing outside her world. She never forgave me for marrying.

It was a hasty marriage and a ponderous mistake, one I paid for many times. Unhappiness breeds the will to die. Only courage and faith keep us safe. Lying in that hospital bed angered that I had wakened at all, I waited that first day for Virginia to come.

When she did, she was with a neighbor. It shocked me to see him there with her. I had assumed she spent the vigil alone. Now it seemed she stood very near to him as though she would leap into his arms the moment I looked away. I cursed God for giving me the life with which to witness this hurt. Was my illness merely an excuse for her to find another man's arms? Did she find this neighbor attractive? I had often thought so. I could not blame her. He was tall, muscular and very good looking, all the things I am not. Why not prefer him to me? Should not those first few moments have been ours? Should we have shared them alone and together? Hadn't my cancer given her the very opportunity to be in his arms? Anger is the corruption of the soul and jealousy the corruption of the heart.

Perhaps she did love him in some little way, I thought. My wife had enjoyed several close relations with male friends. She once got so excited that her kitchen would be renovated in three days she hugged the contractor and kissed him. She seemed capable of intimate though sexually innocent friendships. In the last several years we had quarreled and nearly divorced on several occasions. Her children seemed more important to her than our marriage. Where once I had been the white knight, I no longer held that place in her esteem. It was rare that I awoke to find her in bed in the morning. We quarreled over sex, over discipline for my step son, over temperament and feelings, over training methods for our horses and even over my daily activities—which I now admit bordered on risky but insane. Yes, it was conceivable that she was attracted to him. So much was it conceivable that I contrived a fiction that she was not my wife but the wife of the man standing with her. They had merely come to visit me as a friend.

I did not tolerate anesthetic well. Morphine caused me to hallucinate that I was catching little scissors that were flying past my eyes. The man seemed uneasy. He felt out of place being there at my wife's request. His smile was weak and embarrassed. I smiled at him to relieve his discomfort but even pained as I was, I understood that he was an honorable man who did not believe he should be there at that particular time. I was happy he had supported Virginia in her hour of distress but I was irrational on whether it was right or wrong for him to be there at the first visit.

Again I cursed God for giving me life. At what cost had it come? I could not even bury my dog, nor spend the final moments with her before the earth swallowed her forever. Then the final indignity, to awaken, be alive, see my wife standing close to another man and relive the anguish all over again.

I had been steeped in anger and self pity before the operation.

Over the course of months I deliberately ignored all warning signs. I suffered cramps, constipation, poor digestion. I doubled up so intensely only powerful pain killers afforded me any relief. I thrived on laxatives, sleeping pills and codeine. Weeks before my scoping I passed blood and I knew then that death was tapping on my shoulder.

The woman came every day. The friend did not. I hallucinated that it was generous of him to send his wife to care for me. I wondered if I had a wife. If I did, what was she like? Was she as kind as the woman who visited? There were many days we spoke but the drugs had dulled my recollection. The woman left me at night and then the nights were long and filled with the hospital noises. There is a hush which descends upon the corridors at night and even the swish of a starched nurse's uniform can be heard. Sleep is restless and disturbed with tests and ministrations. It did not matter though because I did not believe I would leave the hospital. I was there to die, not to survive.

I was too ill even to be angry and yet I found anger in myself. I found hatred. I hated the cancer because it failed to strike me down. I hated the illness because I could not see my dog for the last time. I welled up with loathing because another man's wife had to suffer the inconvenience of ministering to me. I had no wife. My children telephoned and refused to believe I was ill. Friends came and in their eyes I saw horror and pity for me. New faces came each day to test and bathe me. Doctors visited me with somber looks and lies on their lips.

Why did they not just tell me I was going to die? Why perform a charade? I could not speak except with a rasp because the tubes had irritated my throat.

One has time to think during the lonely endless hours of the night. Who was this pale, haggard man who stared back at me from the bathroom mirror? His eyes were dull and lifeless. His hair seemed gray, almost white, so when did he grow old? The skin beneath his jaw had grown flabby. Was this the time in his life when his body failed him? If so, how had he survived the surgery? Where did the woman go when she left me? Was my dog really dead? Or had she revived again as she had three times before my hospitalization? Why did the friend not come with his wife? Why did he allow her to live in my home?

The hospital workers brought me food three times each day. I had no stomach for it and I did not eat. The woman offered to bring me food. I refused. Why feed a dead man? For that matter, why care for a dead man at all? Would she not be better off with her husband? And why had she been afraid to hug him in my presence? It seemed she had wanted to, so why not? Affection was natural between husband and wife. Was I the impediment?

They sent me home two weeks later. I was the worse for wear. My incision hurt and the infection within became the infection in the wound itself. My will to live was non existent. I did not expect to awaken. I did not expect to recover. I kept thinking that perhaps they might bury me near Nikki. I languished in the upstairs bed. Daily, my wife removed the dressing, sprinkled antiseptic on the wound and told me it was doing poorly. My disgust was insufferable. I raged at her because she mentioned the infection. Then it was back to the doctor to remove more stitches and clean the wound. I went home again with no will to see another day. I was still angry about Nikki. I was angry because I was bedridden, angry because my wife loved another man, angry because I saw no future and wanted none.

I lay in the bed, steeped in self pity. Angered that I could not bury or mourn my dog. Angered I had survived. I lay there refusing food or drink. I lay there plotting my own demise when I recovered. I wondered if Nikki was warm enough wrapped in her woolen blanket. When well, I would take some bourbon and a bottle of sleeping pills and lay on her grave to die and to keep her warm.

I read little and replied to none of the cards or well wishes I received. In short, I was miserable. My only consolation was sleep; the pain killers assured me of that. My wife doled them out, leaving nothing within my grasp for fear I would overdose. And each time, just before my afternoon nap, that infernal tapping… rap, rap tapping upon the bathroom window.

"What is that damn tapping noise? Can't you keep it quiet around here?" I yelled. Virginia winced but said nothing. There was nothing she could say because she heard nothing. The noise never seemed to occur when she was near. It came sporadically. Just a soft tapping as if something wished to gain admission. I could not rise. I could not view the windows in that portion of the adjoining room which held the whirlpool bath, the shower, sinks and counters and the private toilet. But it came nevertheless. As if dreaming, I heard it ever so faintly and then, more insistently. It drummed through my brain in daylight or in the long night hours when sleep eluded me. It hammered at my sense of understanding that something unknown was out there, and I was powerless to see it, to move, to destroy it.

Virginia continued dressing my wounds and administering to me, putting on socks when I could dangle my legs off the bed or catering to my appetite when I had one. Why did I never see the love there? She looked vaguely like the woman who had visited the hospital with my friend and so I thought of her as his wife but she was not. She was mine. She might have been better off if she had been his. I spoke harsh words to her. Demanded perfection from her. My lunch was overdone. Or cold. When was I getting fresh water? Where was she in the morning when I needed her?

Who was she talking to on the phone? Why couldn't I have some bourbon?

Yet she nursed me without complaint. Her patient, loving eyes told me she withheld her sharp temper out of love and understanding.

The wound improved. The doctor said so. The incision began to close and then became a ragged scar dissecting my navel and dividing my abdomen into two ugly sections. I hated looking at it then as I hate looking at it now. I considered plastic surgery and then decided to leave it as an angry mark. The mark of Cain, I called it. As the wound mended, so did my strength. I was able to walk short distances without pain but, for the most part, my sapped body was weakened and I slept a good deal more than when completely bedridden. And still, just on dozing or waking, that slight tapping kept coming from the bathroom windows. Again, I shouted. "Will you stop that damn noise? Christ what do you do all day but disappear?"

How I now regret the tears that I brought to her eyes.

The first morning I hobbled my way downstairs, Virginia left the room to boil tea and again came that tapping sound, this time from the rear door of our home. I stumbled to the door in my walker but there was nothing there.

"Did you hear that tapping? Did you, damn it?"

"I had the water running. Where did it come from?" Virginia must have wondered if the anesthetic was still in my system.

"Sometimes from the upstairs bathroom window. But just now I heard it from the rear door window."

She nodded but affirmed that only I had heard the gentle fluttering of the angel which haunted me.

Each morning, I awoke to the tapping. I was able to move around in a walker. I searched each corner of the room, investigating closets, drawers, scanning the curtains. Perhaps the wind had rustled them. But there was nothing that could account for the sound.

As in all healing, I grew stronger. My steps became surer, faster. Only one thought pervaded my waking mind. To recover so I could reach a gun and end my misery. What of depression? It strikes, for no apparent reason, with no apparent aim or purpose, with no regard who it devastates or where it leads them. It robs us of happiness. It steals away the joy of living. It imprisons the mirth of a light wind on a sunlit day, the smell of pine, of good earth being turned, of silver creeks and babbling streams cascading over glossy rocks. It renders them meaningless. We awake one morning and suddenly, the world is not such a nice place. We pick at those we love and push them away when they come near. Jealousy is not born of love but of insecurity and therefore I paid Virginia no compliment when I assumed she had an interest in our neighbor. We stress at minor annoyances and perceive all kinds of plots and conspiracies to undermine us. We awaken in the night's midst, frightened and alarmed that something in the dark is there to harm us. Ghosts? Call them by any name but they are the ghosts of depression and old age. Only one thing distracted me from that depression and that was the annoying, irritating, unabashed tapping at the window.

I awoke earlier, waiting for the sound, determined to find the source. I had just finished showering when the sound erupted again. But this time I was right there in the bathroom. There, perched on the windowsill was a brilliant, red cardinal. It rapped its beak upon the glass, then cocked its head and looked at me with quizzical eyes. It turned its head left, then right, but always those smiling, inquiring eyes stared back at me. I walked nearer the window expecting it to fly away. It did not. Instead, it tapped again as if knocking on a door, insistent that it be admitted. It did not hurry away.

There was no food to attract it. Nothing in the room it could want.

It amazed me that this tiny bird had the courage to remain at the window even when I was just inches away. It stared at me as if it knew me. Just a red cardinal, but it came every day.

When I went downstairs for meals, the cardinal came to the rear window and sat on the crossbars, tapping on the window. There was no mistaking its intent. It wanted to enter the house. But what was the bird doing there? What did it want? And why did those eyes remind me so much of Nikki? Was it Nikki? In the questioning arose the will to live just one more day, to discover the truth of who and what this creature was.

One afternoon, I closed off the bedroom door and cracked the window ajar. The cardinal returned. It landed on the window sill and seeing no window to tap upon, hopped from side to side and then flew directly into the bedroom as if it knew exactly where it was going.

I have always slept on the right and Virginia on the left but this bird flew directly to the spot where Nikki used to sleep. It hopped about and stood looking at me as I entered the room. I could have reached out and touched it, so still was that feathered beast. Then, as quickly as it entered, it flew out the open window and across the yard, disappearing into the trees.

The cardinal came every day, and on those days when I opened the window, it flew directly to the place where Nikki had laid. It perched on the comforter and stared with its head cocked and those questioning eyes as if it were a child awed by a sorcerer. In time, I sat on the bed where it perched and at times it even hopped upon my leg, looking up at me as if to say: "Don't you know me? I'm Nikki." Perhaps she was Nikki. Nikki, in another life, another form. Nikki, not dead at all, but risen in another spirit that filled the air with flight and song. If Nikki could live in yet another form, who was I to wrest life from myself and cast it away? Where would I go? What would I become? If this bird were Nikki, then life did not end with death. No, it continued, ad infinitum, into space and dimension and perhaps, with the same pain I felt on earth.

The cardinal continued to visit periodically over the course of five summers, sometimes at the upstairs windows and other times at the rear door. It would not enter a downstairs window, only the bedroom. I often wondered where it went on days I did not see it but that question was never answered. Toward the last days of summer, it flew to my bed and perched there. It tilted its head and stared directly at me. I extended my left hand. It hopped upon it. Then, I enclosed it with the right hand so that it lay within the cup of my grasp.

What little effort it would take to crush this feathered thing? But why? Why would I crush it as I had crushed my wife's spirit? Would I harm it as I had hurt Virginia? Would I repay its kindness, its care, by crushing it to death? Despite all my anger, I was not a cruel person. Why had I been so to my wife? Could I not accept the simple love she offered?

I recalled that God protects all creatures as He tends us. It called to mind meaningful words. So as I held that tiny life in my shaking hands, I mouthed the words: *The Lord is my Shepherd. I shall not want. He maketh me to lie down in green pastures.* Like the cardinal, my wife appeared daily. She tended me, provided company. When I needed to be nursed, she tended my wound. When I slept, she watched over me. At night I heard her praying and knew she prayed for me. She was not my friend's wife but mine. She was a woman who waited while fate decided whether her husband lived or died. Why did I not see her as frightened rather than a seductress? Was I so self centered I could not see that she was afraid? Afraid I might die and she would be alone. Afraid I might die and she would have so many memories to recall. Was she weaker than I thought? Did her resolve fail her when confronted with the reality of my potential death? She told me that every time our friend Vernon stopped talking, she would cry and fall into his arms. But if my jealousy was correct then why did she endure my insult? Why did she nurse me? Why did she pray for my recovery? Why did she never miss a single treatment of my chemotherapy? If she loved another, why did she wait on me almost as a servant while the killing fluids coursed through my body? Why did she tolerate my irritability when the chemicals scorched my brain? Or was she my mother, who never saw a single good in any achievement I made? Was she the mother who stuffed me in a box and imprisoned my heart and mind inside? Was it I who could not accept her love, her loyalty, her pride in me?

He leadeth me beside the still waters.

Had Virginia been my water of life? Had my anger obscured her love?

"Lord, I do not ask to be special to the one I love but rather to accept that love and to understand that it is mine."

Was the problem ever with her? *I shall fear no evil.*

No. I thought. I've lost faith. I have been a selfish, angry child. Cancer was an adult disease and it was time for me to mature. I needed to say the words that showed appreciation, not anger. Whatever occurred in my past, Virginia had no more to do with it than the cardinal. Had I become such an ingrate I could not see Virginia's devotion? Did I not understand that she loved me enough to grant me any request? That all along I had this power of love and did not understand it or accept it? Nor was there any reason Virginia would not put aside her pride and accept my anger and abuse. But that was wrong. She should not be punished for her love.

He restoreth my soul. As Virginia and the cardinal had restored mine.

In the fifth year, I was declared cancer free. The cardinal had come every summer for five years. And like the cardinal, my loyal wife had been there tending me. To celebrate, I purchased expensive champagne for us and special birdseed for my little friend. And my little friend came. It flew to the upstairs window and tapped on the glass. I admitted it and, as was always the case, it flew to the center of the bed where Nikki had laid. Virginia joined me.

"What do you think? Is this Nikki?" she asked.

"I think it's either Nikki or something she sent in her place. I just don't know."

Neither of us knew. Nor will either of us ever know. If it wasn't Nikki then a cardinal came in her place. It came, unafraid, to restore my faith, to give me purpose, to appreciate the wonderful woman who loved me. It came as a symbol of love, to confirm the beauty in the smallest and simplest of creatures. It flew to where Nikki used to snuggle between us, cocked its head, its inquiring eyes staring back at me. *He restoreth my soul... surely goodness and mercy shall follow me all the days of my life...*

"I don't think it will come any more." I whispered.

"Why not? He's come for five years." She answered while watching the bird.

"He's done his work. He had something to teach me. To appreciate love when it is mine. No, I think he will go now."

I was right. The cardinal stayed a little while with us that day. Then it alighted on the windowsill and pecked on the window to be free. I raised the window and stretched a trembling hand to stroke its head. His feathers were soft and warm. I offered it my finger but it would not accept. It gazed directly at me, rolling its head, cocking it side to side. It was as if it were trying to communicate something.

I understood then. He was saying goodbye. He had come to nurse me back to health, to restore my soul and impart love. I nodded. The bird caught the gesture, pecked me gently and moved away. I stepped back. Then, I slid my arm around Virginia's waist and pulled her to me.

"I'm sorry." I said. "I love you. More than that, thank you for loving me." It was my arms into which she fell. My lips she kissed. The tears she shed were for me.

All the cardinal heard and witnessed, then it chirped once, and flew into the wilderness of dimension beyond the window. We never saw it again.

Nonbelievers will accuse me of stretching the
imagination beyond limits.
I assure you I have not lied or bent the truth.
Those of you who visit the Krazyduck.com website
will behold a picture of the very Cardinal
that visited me. It is perched on the
rear door of our home.
How do I know it was Nikki? Faith? Desire?
What bird comes near a human being,
not even a bird in captivity?
What bird seeks admittance
into a home and flies to the very bed
where Nikki napped with us?
And what bird departs
when her message has been delivered
and she is no longer needed?

Russ

The Return Of Lucky

Lucky was already nickering as I started down the frozen, moonlit path to the barn. Lucky whose back had borne ten thousand butts of squealing, squirming children riding the circus pony, whose flanks had borne the kicks and scrapes of ten thousand excited kids, pulling at his mane, yelling in his ear, urging him to go faster in the hot summer sun. Lucky, whose owners had seen my grandfather's love for me and his inexperience with horses and had represented Lucky as seven when he was nearer to twenty-seven. They said he was prone to wheeze in winter, but he weathered the cold weather well if given hay and shelter. In fact the reason they had sold him was because he was old and ill and could work no more. The vet who examined him when Lucky arrived at our farm only shook his head and frowned.

"How could you buy this animal? Look at his feet. His coat. His teeth. This animal is a monument to everything that can go wrong with a pony." But it didn't matter that he was in poor health. My grandfather wanted a happy child and I desperately needed a companion.

When I first saw Lucky at rest he was standing in his stall, knee deep in musty, brown straw. His eyes were dull and lifeless as if he no longer cared. It was as though he had once had great aspirations of the life he should lead and all had proven false. He had a brown and white pinto coat, scruffy and stained from lack of grooming and his hooves were long and untrimmed. His face was mostly brown with a snip of white dead center of his forehead. Two days before he had been carrying children around and around an endless circle, until he no longer needed to watch the circular path. A single day before I had been one of those kicking, squirming children until I saw him standing in the torried sun, with a putrid bucket of water to drink and nothing to eat. There were no children the next day for the circus was closed. I thought of Lucky, living with no will to live. I thought of the days after when he'd pace the endless circle, endure the endless kicks, suffer the bouncing children who pounded on his ragged back. We visited there to purchase a circus pony because I had prevailed upon my grandfather. Because he loved me, he did.

Lucky did not see me when he looked. He had long ago grown used to looking past the children who rode him. It did not matter. Aching, hurting, hiding his hunger and thirst, his boredom, he seldom noticed anyone. Perhaps along the way there had been some kind ones, children with a handful of sugar or cotton candy, but on that day as he stood in his stall racked with a hollow cough, his nose dripping and wet, he paid little noticed to anyone or anything.

Even if he did not see me, I saw him. Small enough for me to mount unassisted and calm enough to be an easy ride, Lucky was the ideal pony for me. I never knew what my grandfather paid for him. For a pony it was probably too much, but for a friend, it was not near enough. Lucky came home to my grandfather's farm, to open fields and briar patched woods, bottomlands with swampy trails and modest ridges. If there was any bond between us, it was that we were both small and both suffered from asthma.

I turned Lucky out into a lush, green pasture, determined that he would have rest. He approached no one, even advancing to his grain bucket with modest caution. In time we would become friends, but for the most part he stood in the furthest part of his field and remained aloof. In time he came for his grain but still maintained his distance, nearing long enough only to eat and then walking determinedly away. I would follow him then, hold out an apple or carrot, feed him and then leave. Most times, I stood quietly away from him and watched. In the passing months, we came to know each other. In time, he even drew closer. Then came the daily treats, deposited first into his bucket, then offered by hand and finally, wonderfully, accepted by an animal whose human contact had taught him to expect anything but good.

In the fields, with the brick farm house nearby, good spring water and robust grains and grasses, Lucky grew stronger. He sprouted a shiny coat to replace the long, dull hair of yesterday. Even his ribs disappeared, one by one and then, a slight plumpness invaded. When I approached him then, his eyes were clear and bright, deep brown pools of soul that reached far inside him and told me he was wondering about his new life, his new friend.

Grooming began slowly, using first a small towel and then a brush. Lovingly I slid my hands over his smooth, satin coat. I moved them up and over his ears, then down between his eyes where I scratched. At first there were things I did not understand, as when he nuzzled me with his nostril, blowing warm breath into my own nose. Later, I understood it was his way of saying hello, of offering his friendship and his trust. There is no pride or satisfaction more worthy than when an animal bestows his trust.

Farm hands laughed and teased that I was afraid to ride him. Since I had never ridden I did not know if it was fear or patience that kept me from it. Perhaps he had faced his fears and I had not. Or perhaps he counseled me in the ways of patience that I had never known. Summer wore on. For some reason, my allergies seemed to have abated and he, too, no longer wheezed and puffed when he paced the fence line. I earned his trust and groomed him every day, rubbing his coat until it glowed with spirit.

It was on such a day I straddled the paddock fence, watching him demolish the last of his grain. He did not turn and saunter off as he usually did. Instead, he circled again and again and then came right to the fence where I was sitting. He sidled next to me, pushing his flank against my leg. When I remained inert, he nuzzled my leg with his nose and gazed at me with brown, confident eyes as if to say: "I can carry you safely. You've no need to fear." The eyes no longer appeared sad or disillusioned.

It was natural that my leg should flow easily over his back. Then I was mounted, with no saddle or bridle. Expectation streamed over me. He did not move immediately but waited until I was settled and balanced on his back. I gripped his sides with my legs and held onto his mane, for I had no idea what he would do. He took a slow step forward, then another and yet another. Slow, easy pace, around in a small circle, then widening the circle until we traversed the entire length of the fencing and returned to the original point. My fears paled. He tramped away slowly. Not a single misstep or a single quick step. It was as though he was a circus pony again and I was a squirming, squealing kid. But I was not. I was his friend. And he was mine.

We were one that day. One in a way of bonding, of friendship.

If my balance slipped a little, Lucky moved under me like a safety net. If I leaned too far one way or the other, he placed himself fully under me. We traveled the paddock again and again until I relaxed and flowed along with him. I do not know how long we rode that day. Long enough for my mother to shriek that I would be killed and to demand abdication from my friend's back. Lucky reacted stoically. He'd heard nagging mothers before.

And so the magic ended until the next time mom was away and Lucky and I could ride again.

I learned the use of saddle pad and saddle. Learned to place the bit kindly into his mouth. When mother watched, we rode only in the paddock. But when she was away, we slipped out through the gate and down the long lane to the cow pasture in back of the farm. It was an open grazing area bordered by woods; beyond lay swamps and tangles and marshes and woodland ponds of brackish water and clear running brooks. Beyond it laid the freedom of the wetlands, freedom from illness, from school bullies who chided me over my small stature, from doctors who endlessly probed and stuck and tested.

Mother was always there to censure. Grandfather and sometimes dad, to defended and cajole. She did not take to Lucky but then she took to little in my life. Lucky understood that and ignored her demanding screams. Yet, together we found freedom in each other. Each winter brought its bronchial pneumonia, bouts of breathlessness, days of delirious fever. Time without Lucky was endless and yet, my dream of being with him again steadied me to recover. What is there to live for if not the hope that yearns within us? It erupted in Lucky when we found each other and it erupted in me because of Lucky. Otherwise life was merely one bedroom prison after another with no tomorrow.

Thus, on that day before the winter set, on that early morning jaunt down the frozen, moonlit path, Lucky was waiting, waiting as if we both understood that this would be last ride for a long time. For winter had come early and we were still at the farm. The damp air caught deep in my lungs. Each breath tightened a band around my chest. Each cough was raspier than the last. But that hope of which I spoke leapt forth like a staunch spirit and drove me forward. It would only be a matter of days before Lucky and I were separated.

Lucky, too, was snorting and wheezing but his eyes were bright and he was impatient for us to be gone. If this time was freedom for me, it was freedom for him as well.

I smeared his bit with apple and saddled him. We slipped quietly from the barn, down the long, frozen lane and into the back paddock.

The open sky was vivid and glistening, pocked with stars and dark, still clouds. A breeze blew up from the east and along with it the earthy smell of manure from cattle that had dwelled there.

We stopped for a time, me to admire the night and Lucky to graze on the long grass not eaten by the cows. We rode on to an icy brook where we both paused to drink. We moved on again. We plied the deer trails, trod through the sullen woods and traversed carefully through shallow, frozen ponds to what lay beyond. There is no mystery greater than the next hill or next glen, no excitement more scintillating than the discovery of unfamiliar lands. I do not think in all the time we rode we ever went into the woods the same way or came out in the same place.

But that was part of the freedom. No matter where we went, Lucky always knew how to take me home. Once home, the freedom was ended. Mom scowled and forbade me to ride again and whisked me inside to bundle me up in wool blankets that suffocated me. There was only the dream of freedom. Sometimes it was days before she turned me out again and then only under her watchful eye. I know dad wished he could intervene but he was not strong and so he stayed silent. I was young but old enough to know I hated dad's weakness. Unlike other boys who emulate their fathers, I avoided any resemblance to him. Until Lucky, dad was my only hope for freedom. Regrettably he failed me. The only strength remaining was the hope she would return to our city home. When she did, I was free if only for a little while.

We started again at a slow walk, trying to gain some distance before mom knew I was gone. I had never spirited away in the dead of night. She'd be furious if she discovered me gone. Lucky understood this now and hurried his steps, slipping just a little on the frozen ground. The winter frost had come much earlier than usual and we were usually the first to be affected when winter struck. For Lucky and I, winter was always arduous. My nose clogged up and congestion ruled my chest. Fever came upon fever and breath was hard to come by. For months, I lay in bed, reading the same books over and over, playing with the tiny metal soldiers who were my friends. Doctors came sticking long, silver needles into my ears to remove congestion and still others administered the awful tasting sulfur.

And for Lucky, it was no better. He fought his own battle with heaves and pneumonia. The vet had said he would not last the year. Indeed neither of us might. Thus before our freedom ended, we went treading down the lane to the rear pasture and, once out of sight, were free to roam at will. I planned on returning just before dawn so mom would never know. We crossed the pasture and touched the edge of the woods. It swallowed us with welcoming arms and we were bonded with the land and the wind. Once inside, we were safe from mom's purview.

Lucky sneezed, a hard, head-shaking sneeze while I had a slight sniffle and then both of us in sequence were racked with a minor cough. A child of six who has always coughed, always suffered congested lungs and nostrils, who has always wheezed and hacked through every winter and every damp day, does not understand that in horses this is not a normal event. It was the exhilaration that drove us and thus we ignored the cold and the damp and the chill. Along the streams were the tracks of the night animals, gray and red foxes, bobcat, deer, raccoons, rabbits, weasels, all written in the snow where Lucky and I read the book of life. And in that book were the stories of life and death struggles that unfolded on the very ground we rode. A winter hare darted into the hidden brush. A deer startled off, leaving only its sound of flight. The night was clear and we were free, linked as only a young child and his horse can be.

It was a land asleep, covered with the blanket of white fleece that softened all sound. Even crashing branches, falling from the overladened burden of heavy snow, did not disturb the quiet. We crossed small streams, now crusted with thin ice, then headed up the low ridges to the top where cedar and hemlock trees huddled together.

Where there were deer trails, we trailed along them and traced the paths nature had formed. All was still. Where the path ended, blocked by a windfall, we wove around it. It endowed me with a satisfaction of riding in places where no other rider had ever been. We circumvented trees that blocked our path and backtracked where we could not. Lucky was as sure-footed as if he had been born a woodland animal. Time was frozen like the land. We meandered along hidden trails and where there were none, we sculpted them again and again. There is a nearness to the Creator when one traipses the woods as if God's home is in the forest. One ponders life's meaning, whether trees and plants have sensitivity, whether we pass from this world into the next, whether my next bout with pneumonia would be my last, would I ever be free of mom, how long would Lucky be part of my life. Would I have friends? Would there be other such rides in solitude? Would the quiet always be my friend? Would the dark always frighten me?

Yes, even a child can ponder such questions. Lucky and I traveled in silence. Only our wheezing and coughing broke the silence. I hated when the air rattled in and out of my chest. Hated when the mold clamped shut my lungs. But Lucky plodded on and I with him. It is not often boy and animal are one.

If Lucky could have spoken, what would he have said? Would he have spoken of the trails and somber forest, so free, so unencumbered by humanity? Would he have expressed relief at the freedom from screaming children? No buckets of warm, cloudy water. No dried out hay. No plodding around the same, interminable circle, day after day in suffocating sun. Breathing the dust into his scarred lungs. Would he have enjoyed freedom from filthy wagons and small trailers- - the jarring endless rides from one circus to another? Was he happy to venture out into the forest? Would I always be his friend? Would he one day have to find another home? Or would he simply have sighed?

The wind blew cool. Dark gray hands crossed the sky and when it darkened, more snow swept down in tiny rivulets and in curling gushes like grass bending before the wind. Lucky labored on, his steamy breath escaping like the gasp of some huge locomotive. My own chest was tightened and so I labored as did Lucky. Yet, the woodland mystique incarcerated us just a moment longer, and another and another and yet another. There were many acres on my grandfather's farm, and many days until summer again. Neither of us wanted to return.

Mother was sure to punish me for my indiscretion. As in all things she protected me by denying me the things I most loved. Lucky and the farm would be no exception. She would take Lucky away and make certain I never saw him again. Dad might raise a small objection but she'd ignore him. Grandfather would earn me no reprieve for he respected her authority over me. There is no reprieve from life; it binds us to what we are and who controls us. It binds us just as surely as the bit and reins bound Lucky to what he was.

We stopped on a hilltop, hoping to glimpse some familiar site. There was only snow: snow on the hills, in the branches, on the trails we had followed, even covering the creeks and blotting out the water. I dismounted on a ridge and from my saddle bag produced a small sack of grain and some crackers. This was our snack, the whole of it. I cupped my hands and held the grain. Lucky brushed my face with his nose before eating. I nuzzled him with my own. He ate slowly and wheezed as he did so. When done, I ate the last crackers and took up a hand full of snow for moisture. As I stared upward, the sky was black and deadly. The moon was lifeless. Daylight was not far away. It hid behind the huge wads of white swirled on wind currents like debris in a wind tunnel. It was time to return, time to surrender the freedom.

When I mounted again, my short legs stretching to catch the stirrups, I was feverish and Lucky's wheeze seemed ever worse. I knew then we were both sick, so sick I could not control his movements so I loosened the reins and asked him to head home. He understood home.

He labored through the white fluff, scarring it with his hoof prints. The wind cut against us and made us both shiver. The sky lightened as day approached but the snow did not abate. It soaked into us like heavy water, dousing us to the skin. When all was hopeless, there still was Lucky's confident path home. Two hours later, Lucky stumbled up to the barn. We were both quaking with cold but he walked into his stall and stopped. The absence of wind felt good.

I unsaddled him and toweled the dampness from his shaggy coat. After watering him, I offered him his hay and feed but he did not eat. He lay down in the warm hay. I sat beside him for I was exhausted too. Lucky's nose was running and he felt hot. The fever rose up in him and it rose up in me. My ears stung. My face burned. As I lay against his heaving body, I slipped into a troubled sleep.

I do not know when day came. I only felt strong arms lift me and carry me away. I did not see Lucky lying there nor say goodbye. I only felt the warmth of bedding and the comfort of home. The blankets snugged up around me and loosened my chest. While the doctor ministered to me, easing my cough, easing my breath, a vet ministered to Lucky. We both struggled for our lives yet neither knew of the other's struggle. Nor would either of us have altered anything if we had. In my tortured fever I rode him again. This time the frozen trails had no beginning and no end and the cold had no bite. The woods were picturesque and tranquil in a world without worry or pain. Lucky was no longer a circus pony but a trail horse. And for a brief time, I was a man, independent and determined.

There is no sleep without breath, neither for me nor for Lucky. My ears clogged and pained me. Fluid clogged my chest. I wondered if Lucky was still sleeping in his stall. I wanted him well, to see him again, perhaps to steal a ride when mother went away. But mom stayed. She would not risk the journey into the city because of the storms. The doctors came and went. They plied me with sulpha drugs and needles. They bribed me with broken promises I would not be hurt. The medicines did little good and their promises were as empty as their treatments.

Weeks later, I regained enough strength to peer out the bedroom window. Lucky was not grazing in his usual place. The land was still a winter blanket of snow and ice. I searched for hoof prints in the snow but there were none. I returned to bed, too weak to remain standing. When I asked about Lucky, eyes turned away and voices lowered and eyes avoided my gaze. But no one spoke of him except to say he was resting.

When Spring came, the rage in my chest and head ceased. The pounding pain in my ears subsided. I was permitted two hours a day by the window to enjoy the sunlight. But I still could not see Lucky in his paddock and still, no one would meet my eyes when I asked about him. Had mom finally convinced grandfather to part with Lucky? That thought drove me into desperation. I had to know where he was. I wondered why I had to fear my own mother. Wondered why dad was not strong enough to protect me.

On the day I was strong enough to walk, I tottered haltingly to the barn to look for Lucky. Would he even remember me? Accept the carrot I held for him? Nicker as he always did?

But he did not nicker. He was not in his paddock or in his stall. Even the saddle and bridle were gone. There was only the worn leather halter he wore, the one we had never replaced. No hay, no bedding, just a broom clean stall, empty and unused. Nor was he in the fields or anywhere except the place where good horses go when they are dead. There is a sickness that rises in the stomach when such expectations are not met. My breath was drawn in frightened sobs as I searched for my friend. I paced back and forth within the barn. I hiked the field looking for a sign of him. But there was none. Lucky had fought the same fight as I, but he had lost. It was his age, the vet said. They put him down and buried him in the paddock where he had lived. His resting place was an unmarked grave.

I never asked for another pony. My grandfather bought one, but it was not mine. Lucky was mine. This new pony would be nothing to me but another horse. He and I eyed each other but never grew to be friends. Perhaps he was a nice horse. I do not know. I had no desire to be his friend. A broken heart finds no consolation in substitution, nor does memory find any release from what love has made immortal. In time we left the farm. Grandfather died and grandma periodically sold off parcels of land to sustain herself.

I declared war on mom. It was a silent war that transcended time. She would not dominate me. She would never deprive me of anything again. It was not so much a clash of words as a clash of wills. Whatever she bade me to do, I did the opposite. I defied her at every turn. I proved myself stronger, more vigilant than my father. It was not a war of spite but of independence. There are times, though, when I wonder who really won the battle for the scars accompanied me into adulthood.

Peace finally came when she laid complaining and whining on her death bed. She scolded my sister for bringing her there but when she saw me, her face glowed with a rarely seen happiness. We talked for hours. The anger within me subsided. I realized that she had no other way to love me but to be overprotective and I could no longer hate her because her love was misdirected. Just before she slipped away, she whispered, *"Take care of yourself sonny. I love you."* I held her hand until it grew cold. She passed as suddenly as dad. I kissed her gently on the cheek.

"Take care of yourself, sonny," she cried again. This was the woman who accused me of diverting her Social Security and her private retirement funds when she was living with my sister in New Jersey and I was settled in Kentucky. Then the light in

her eyes glazed and became dull. Something left her. Life left her. She did not move again. The war was ended. I was independent and alone. All the years we had fought, ignored one another, avoided contact, and clashed disappeared in a few hours. She had forgiven me my obstinate path. I had forgiven her the tough love she enforced. Love isn't always tender and kind. But it's love nonetheless.

Suddenly forty years had passed bringing with it a law career, politics and two marriages. I had little enough time for other things but managed some travel. On my dresser stood the only memory of Lucky and me that survived my busy lifestyle… a single photo of me mounted on the brown and white pony. Although I'd seen the photograph a hundred times, I'd never noticed him smiling. But he was. Why had I never seen his happiness?

And then as if resurrecting that lost memory I accepted an invitation to trail ride in the mountains of Taos, New Mexico, a scenic ride across native American lands. "Therapeutic, healthful," my friends said. What did they know of Lucky?"

We saddled up near Pueblo and rode for most of the day. Although the land was lovely, trails were narrow and sometimes treacherous. I spent most of my time holding the horn and wishing I had not come. Then it was dusk, and the Indian guided us to our encampment. Tranquil, lavender hues of the mountain desert washed softly over us. They mounded huge logs into a teepee and ignited them. Flames lashed the black sky and drove it back as they swept upward. The camp was brightly illuminated with its crackling light. It was said of travelers to this enchanted land that time ended there and those who visited stepped into the past and became one with it. But I thought, in my skeptical way, that it was the altitude making everyone giddy.

The fire was warm and my bones were sore from the long ride. I leaned against a rock and let the warmth work its magic. The questions I had asked on my woodland rides as a child no longer plagued me. Instead other questions filled my mind and then scurried before the chilly night air and the comforting fire. I thought of mom; I was happy we had made peace and I understood that she had loved me in a very strange way, but she had loved me nonetheless. I wished her love had been as warm and comforting as the fire. In the end it was enough that the love had been there.

In moments, I dozed. When I awoke the fire was still burning and the moon, still full. A coyote summoned from a high mesa. I searched to see if he was outlined by the moonlight but he was not. The other riders had long since gone to their bedrolls. I stretched out my legs and shifted. It was cozy here. Even the rock at my back seemed comfortable and reassuring. As I drifted off again, a nicker reached my ears. It startled me because our trail horses were some distance away. At first I saw nothing but the fire and its burnished perimeter. The nicker came again, more familiar then. I peered into shadows, studying the shapes and sizes of ghosts that lay at the fire's edge. And that was where he stood. A small brown and white pony, a white snip dead center of his forehead. Lucky gazed at me with bright, confident eyes that seemed to say, "We will ride again when its time." My throat constricted. Tears forged up. I rubbed my eyes clear of their mist because reason would not accept the vision of truth standing there. I closed my eyes for a brief time. When I looked again, he was gone.

I knew then that forty years had not passed at all. Lucky had been waiting on the other side of life. One day, I will climb the mesa where Lucky has gone and he'll be waiting still, waiting for his friend, waiting to be joined again in the dwelling that now separates us and waiting to ride into the celestial light.

How fortunate are those of us,
Whose friends await them near the hill.
Whose shadowed forms are ever near.
Whose constant love is never still.

Russ

Empty Nest

It was an act of defiance. I admit that now. Being twenty, a college student, earning his own pay at full time work, I was entitled to be defiant. Earning one's pay renders a sense of power that may not in fact exist when a mother is domineering and restrictive.

Not that fate didn't play a part. I spent a few idle hours before work began and decided to visit the Farmer's Market in Newark. I wasn't looking for anything in particular. The Farmer's Market was just an interesting place, full of sounds and industry, trucks rumbling over cobblestone streets, crates slamming against the concrete docks, roughened oaken doors creaking on weathered hinges, men bellowing the sale of fruits and vegetables, horse drawn wagons backing up to loading ports, even the slapping of fresh fish against ice. I often went there simply to browse and perhaps watch the live crabs scurrying around their containers.

On this occasion, though, the sound of cheeping roused my curiosity. I could not resist. There, in the window of the poultry dealer turned pet store, were chicks and ducks being sold for Easter, novelty items for children. Most died long before Easter while the survivors found their way back to the same poultry butcher. But that thought was distant. I was feeling both lonely and defiant and determined to buck my strong willed mother by purchasing a duck.

One duck in particular struck my favor. Most chicks and ducks were clustered near the center of the display, some splashing in and out of the water pan, others jabbing at the grain set in a long, metal trough.

But the one I fancied stood forlorn and abandoned in a far corner. I always prefer the underdog. His down was scruffy. His eyes dull. He stood sleeping on one leg until jostled by two chicks and then, he waddled off into another lonely corner. Somehow we made eye contact. I knew, then, that he was the duck for me.

The store owner had little to do and seemed friendly enough. A rotund, diminutive man with amiable eyes and thick features, he wiped his hands and leaned into me, almost whispering.

"You don't want that duck," he said. "He won't last a day or two. Pick a more active one, say, like" he pointed to two or three at the water dish. "See how their eyes are bright and alert. They'll survive just about anything. They don't need much anyway. Just some food, water and a warm place to live. But Christ, don't place them by the stove or the gas fumes will kill them. Every year I have to listen to some little kid tell me the sad story of how he put his chick by the stove to keep it warm and how it died and could he have another chick. So what am I gonna do when all the chicks are gone?"

"I don't know. I kind of like that little guy."

"He shouldn't even be in the window. My partner bought this lot. I guess he didn't spot him."

"How much are they?"

"Chicks are two dollars. Ducks are 3.50."

"And the sick one, how much for him?"

"Determined to have that one, huh? Well, I got to sleep nights so I'll take a buck for him."

"It's not that I don't appreciate your advice. You're probably right. But he's an underdog. Nobody wants him. Everybody kicks him around. Reminds me of myself. Yeah, I'll take him."

"All sales are final. If he dies as you walk out the door, no returns." He cocked his head sideways as if to emphasize the point.

"Good enough. Now, there must be something I can do to make him well?"

"Keep him warm. Feed him in small portions, maybe. The other ducks have been knocking hell out of him around the grain bin. Felt sorry for him but I can't keep these things very long. Got to move them."

"Do they have vitamins for ducks? Anything like that?"

He shrugged and shot me an incredulous look. "Uh, I don't think so. Build him a little nest in a box where it's warm. Maybe he'll make it with food and water. Scraggly little guy."

He boxed the duck in a cardboard container. Occasionally it poked its bill out through one of the air holes and emitted a quack. I couldn't take it to work with me so I stopped at Joey Head's place and asked if he could keep it for me. Actually his name was Joey Giordano but they called him "Head" because his head size exceeded all reasonable proportions to his body. He had a heart to match though.

They could have called him Rubber Lips too, because they seemed thick and swollen as if he had hung weights on them. His hair was black, kinky and greased with pomade. He was the only kid in Downneck Newark who had failed kindergarten twice. It wasn't that he was stupid; it just took a while for things to get from his ears to his brain.

"Keep yer duck? Ya want me to keep yer duck? Do I look like a zoo keeper?" He laughed. Joey always laughed at his own jokes. Among friends he was the clown, the dufus. No one took him seriously. Girls mocked and teased him. Little kids quipped about the size of his head. Yet, if someone needed a favor, it was Head who was always there. Squat, square and muscular, he could easily have inflicted violence on those who scoffed at him. But he didn't. He was just always level, good natured, Joey Head.

"Just 'til I finish work. I need to put him in a big box, make a nest for him, and give him some food and water. Got a box around?"

"Yer mother will hit the friggen ceiling when you bring this quacker home, ya know that don't ya?"

"Let me tell you, Joey. I'm twenty. I go to school. I work. I pay my room and board —and more. I'm always out so I don't eat home much. She got rid of my dog but this is my duck and I've got rights too. But I know this animal won't make it past tonight if I bring him there and don't stand around while she gets used to the idea."

He craned his neck and conjured a look that told me he didn't think my rights would stand up against my mother's iron rule.

"I'll take the little bug. Ya can pick him up tomorra. I'll treat him nice; make a nice paper bed in a box. I got water dishes but what'll I feed him?"

I handed him a small bag of grain. "Grain. Ducks love it. Or bread soaked in milk so it's soft. Little pieces."

"A duck! Ya got a duck for a pet!" he marveled, shaking his head as his lips shook. "Russell, you look fer trouble."

"He's a cute little guy. Sleeps most of the time. He won't be much trouble." I commented.

"Go on! See ya tomorra." He waved.

"I'm off work tomorrow around nine."

I gave the duck a farewell look and headed out to work.

Next morning, Joey was waiting for me. He had fashioned a cardboard box and stuffed it with newspaper. In one corner he stacked cotton and in the other, a water tray and food dish. The bird looked more active than the day before.

"He looks better today." I said.

"Yeah." He smiled.

"What?"

"I took 'im to the chicken doctor."

Wary. "Chicken doctor?"

He nodded. "Chicken doctor. He takes care of birds. I had me a parakeet and it was sick. I took 'im to this guy and he gives him some medicine. It worked. So I took yer bird to 'im. He said it was mal… mal… mal something… like he ain't et enough."

"Malnutrition?"

"That's what. The chicken guy says the other ducks was keepin' 'im away from the food. They do dat sometimes. Sometimes, he says, they peck it to death." From a drawer he pulled out a small bottle with an eye dropper. "He says to give him one drop a day in his water."

I could have brought the duck home the day before but I knew better than to shock mom by having her find the duck there without some explanation. I motored home, hoping for a chance to talk to her. Talking to mom always depended on her mood. Generally, it was bad. But some days it was terrible. She was sitting at the table, drinking tea and reading the News. She hardly gave me a look but her eyes pierced the box with x- ray vision. "What the hell do you have now?" It was obviously one of her bad days.

"A duck." I said, as if it were the most common thing in the world. "Well, a duckling actually. I bought him at the Farmer's Market. Want to see him."

"Where the hell are you going to keep a duck? Are you crazy? This is a small house. He'll stink up the whole place."

"The farmer told me he wouldn't. Not if I change his bedding, food and water every day. He'll only take a little room in the box. I won't let him loose."

"He'll crap all over the place."

I hated when she took that tone. Her airs were high and mighty but her speech, low cast. From her, I inherited my short stature, but not her aquiline nose or sculptured features. She was tiny, always inclined toward being overweight but the most remarkable thing about her physically were the veins that popped out in her legs. She had to have them stripped every once in a while or she couldn't stand for long.

"You know, mom, I work hard. I bust my tail in school. I break my back at the A & P Bakery. I sweat blood for my paycheck and you get three-fourths of it…"

"I pay your car payment and your insurance." She shrieked.

"That doesn't equal my pay. And I don't complain. But if this is my house too, I'm entitled to have a pet. You got rid of Palsy. What harm can a duck do?"

"They're filthy and they carry disease. I was just reading an article on chickens and ducks carrying some kind of virus. You think I want that kind of thing growing in my house?"

"Mom, it will only be for a few months. Then I'll keep it in the back yard. No one ever goes back there. It won't cause any trouble."

"I'll talk to your father about it. He won't like it."

"Dad never objects to anything I do, mom. Not unless you tell him to."

"You disrespectful snot!" she screeched. "Keep your God dam little duck. See if I care."

With that, she nosed into her newspaper and ignored me.

"Can't you ever let me have something?"

She continued reading the newspaper.

"I don't ask much, mom."

Silence.

"Okay, so don't talk to me."

With that, I walked to the larger kitchen toward the rear of the house. We lived in a basement, frame home. The kitchens were actually in the basement. We took meals in the smaller, front kitchen unless company was coming. If the company was family we ate in the rear kitchen. If they were high society we ate in the parlor upstairs. One could always tell their status with my mother by where we ate dinner.

I settled the box under the rear sink which ran about half the length of the room. We never used the sink but it had been designed to wash and rinse clothing. At the rear of the room, three steps brought one to a small landing, large enough for two comfortable chairs. This was enclosed with opaque glass as if it had been designed as a hot house of some type. A single door led to a very small back yard. What I liked most about the room were the two pillars which came down onto a ledge. I could lay on the floor, propped up by the ledge which also served as a table for midnight snacks. Evenings, after work, I watched the late show while I drank tea and nibbled on whatever happened to be available. Mom didn't leave dinner for me, so it was mostly banana or ketchup sandwiches and sometimes, unsweetened chocolate.

The duckling seemed perkier when I looked in on him. I set out his water dish with a drop of medication and tapped in a little grain for him to eat. For good measure, I added a drop to his grain. Then, he tapped my hand with his bill, a weak tap, as if he didn't have the strength to really peck. His down was yellow fluff and his eyes had brightened. Even his movements seemed more energetic as he perused his dwelling. He still had that look in his eye which captivated me. Somehow he seemed to be thanking me for giving him a home.

I procured a larger, stronger box, one high enough to contain him. Each day when I left him to attend work or school, it was always with remorse that I might not find him there when I returned. It wasn't unlike things to disappear when mother disapproved. I had delved into hypnotism until one by one, all books had disappeared. Then, I subscribed to a writing course until mother notified the school that at sixteen, I was unable to Contract without parental consent. The instructors cancelled my enrollment. And then there was Palsy, my little Pomeranian, who suddenly developed a rare disease and had to be sent to a warmer climate. In more human terms, there was also my very first romance, Marie. At seventeen, every love is an important one. But Marie and I were not to be. As she told me on parting, I was destined for law and a Judgeship and had to educate my brother and two sisters. I couldn't be involved with an uneducated girl who would work in a factory, marry and live an average life. I thought she made amazingly good sense for a young girl and wondered what prompted her to be so concerned about the future of my siblings and myself. Years later, I met her again and discovered the truth. Mom had interfered… and, it wasn't for the last time.

But each day I returned and Crazy Duck was still there, quacking softly in his abode. He grew quickly and filled out. He was able to leap over the top of the box and so, at bedtime, I covered it with netting. I knew what it would mean if mom caught him roaming. Thursdays, my day off, were visiting days. I brought Crazy Duck to Joey Head's. I freed him from the box and let him wander around the bedroom. The duckling waddled around the room, then spurted to the other side, then poked into things, tapping them with his bill. Then, he hopped into the air and flapped across the room. Several times he tried flying up onto Joey's bed but kept falling short. He seemed unabashed at his failure and would try several more times until he exhausted himself. We fashioned a small nest for him on Joey's bed and let him sleep. Each day we visited Joey, Crazy Duck came nearer reaching the bed, evidence he was growing. His quacks were more pronounced. He wandered longer. His spurts across the room were faster. More importantly, he seemed to bond with Joey and me as if he imprinted us as his parent.

"Yer a daddy." Joey commented.

"And you're a godfather." I laughed.

When we turned our attention to Crazy Duck, he was posed, center of the room, quacking at the two of us, a joke he undoubtedly enjoyed.

My reception at home was seldom good. Every time I walked past the front kitchen with the box, mom's disapproval rating registered a ten.

"When are you going to get some sense in that head of yours? You can't keep that animal here. If you spent as much time on your studies as you do with that duck, you'd be an A student."

"I've got a B average and I'm working full time. I work ten hours a day, attend school another six not including travel time, study two hours and sleep the rest. I don't date. I don't have many friends. Why don't you just put me in jail and release for me school and work?"

"Don't you get flip with me! I'll slap your face."

"Yeah, mom," I drawled, "like you held my hand over the stove because you thought I went in your purse."

"I didn't really burn you. But don't you ever dare go in my purse again."

"I never did in the first place. The damn thing opened up on its own. I heard the snap give."

She looked away, refusing to meet my gaze.

I walked down the corridor to the rear kitchen and set the box in its appointed place. I strapped the netting on so Crazy Duck was contained and left to do some research. At four o'clock, I punched the clock and started into the long, sultry night's work at the bakery. Work by the ovens was exasperating. In winter, the temperature stabbed at 135 degrees. No windows were opened because any reduction in the oven heat affected the baking process. In summer, men died there. The thermometer could not register the heat; it just did not go that high. The grey uniforms we wore rotted from sweat within three or four weeks. Perspiration gushed like river flood. We drank ice cold lemonade made in five gallon buckets and the more we drank, the more we sweated. Every hour a supervisor came by and handed out salt tablets.

But that was work. It paid well. It took its toll. When twelve-thirty a.m. signaled the end of the long day, I punched my card and left the sooty red building totally exhausted. Even the eighty-degree summer evening felt cool and refreshing as I drove home.

The house was asleep when I arrived. It was seldom that anyone was awake. With the bedrooms two floors above the kitchen, I unwound in front of the television, having a snack to signify the end of my toil. Under the stairs beneath the sun parlor, I stowed a bottle of Old Overholt. Each evening, as I lay before the television set, propped against a small pillow, I poured a cup of tea and laced it heavily with whiskey. It helped ease the pain. I turned Crazy Duck loose and let him wander, closing off the kitchen door so he could not escape the room. As he grew older, he negotiated the stairs and sidled next to me, often lying on the cushion.

Being half asleep, I hardly noticed what he was doing until one evening his quack sounded more like a gargle. I glanced down to see him dipping his bill into the whiskey laced tea. It was so humorous, I just watched. Evidently the duck was a boozer. I thought, at first, he'd sip a little and then stop. But the duck liked good rye and kept tapping the cup. I turned back to the movie and lost sight of him until I heard his quack turn to a distress call. When I looked, he was posed on the top step, teetering on the brink. Then, in slow motion, his lopsided body rolled in a slow somersault until he landed on the bottom step, but his body wedged in a corner and he was too drunk to move. He was too drunk to extricate himself so his feet simply walked in the air. All the time, he was wedged there his quack was subdued and melancholy. There are nights when I still see him hopelessly stuck in the corner, his huge body too bottom heavy for his feet to free him and his quacking distress call signaling his dilemma. At such times, Crazy Duck is an essential part of my recollection and I love him for the affection he afforded as well as the companionship he offered.

I lifted him gently from the step.

"Duck," I pronounced. "You're drunk. No more for you tonight."

With that, I tucked him into his bed, pulled some paper over him to shield him from noise and light and left him to sleep it off.

Joey Head publicized the story of the drunken duck and Crazy Duck achieved a certain notoriety. Other boys I had seen around but never socialized with came to see the marvelous drinking duck. On those occasions, I would brew some tea, lace it with a touch of Overholt, and demonstrate his drinking abilities. Crazy Duck never disappointed. He downed his whiskey like a western cow hand. Afterwards, he staggered in a drunken stupor until he found a comfortable spot to rest. Then, he slowly sagged to the floor.

But the duckling was no more a fledgling. His yellow down molted into white. His feet grew larger. His bill became powerful enough to deliver a mighty clout. No more could he be confined to a box but explored instead most of the kitchen. He became more curious, poking and prodding things with his bill. He searched under the radiator. It wasn't unusual to see him with a dust ball clinging to his head. My late night snacks were a thing of the past since he not only imbibed anything I put in a tea cup but pecked at my sandwiches as well.

"You know, duck, we're running out of room. I have to do something with you. Maybe a farm or a petting zoo. Don't worry! Not the butcher. I can't believe how fast you grew. Mom won't stand for this much longer and I can't keep you caged all the time. It's not fair to you. But I'll miss you, duck. I don't have time for friends, and I don't do well with girls. You ever get lonely, duck? I mean, do you ever miss other ducks?"

"Quack."

"I guess not. Nothing seems to bother you. You're always so calm. Even when mom chases you with the broom, you don't seem flustered."

"Quack."

"I get lonely. I see these movies and wish I had a girl. Ever had a crush on a girl? I mean. A girl duck? No, you were too young. All you've ever seen is me. No other ducks."

"Quack. Quack."

"It's been nice having a friend to come home to. We kind of form a nest here, don't we? I mean you and I could have a nest right here. But now, you've outgrown the nest. Funny how that happens. A few years back I was riding a bicycle. Now, I drive a car, pay my bills, attend school, work, and support the family, including a duck. Now that's progress."

"Quack, quack, qia, qua, qua, quack."

"I guess some day I'll have to leave the nest too. This is my nest here. I have a small bedroom upstairs and this is my little corner down here when no one's awake." I sighed a little.

"Quaaaaaccccckkkk."

"Okay, I'll feed you. But what good's a buddy if he won't give you advice or listen to you?"

Loneliness is a powerful stimulant. Otherwise, why would a twenty year old youth adopt a duck as friend and pet? By the time I was seventeen, my mother had engineered so many rejections from the girls I was attracted to that, like Quasimodo, I wondered why I could not be turned to stone.

Crazy Duck accompanied me when I cruised around the City. And he was loyal company when I sat writing assignments for college. When I bought a duck call and began speaking to him, he tilted his head and listened as if he understood. Then he quacked his answer, though I did not understand a single word of duck speak. He was the friend I confided in. He was the companion who was always happy to see me. In return, I cleaned his cage diligently, disinfecting it each night and vacuuming the loose fluff he molted.

There were nights I fell asleep with him cuddled in my armpit. It was then I learned that ducks do snore and dream. Many times I heard him snoring softly and I often observed his feet moving as if he were chasing something in his slumber. I also knew his days with me were numbered. He was almost full grown and need more space and fresh air.

I knew I had to do something with Crazy Duck. He was grown. It was harder and harder to clean up after him. He found new and insidious ways to escape his box. I thought of housing him in the back yard but there were cats and raccoons roaming during the night and I knew he would not be long alive if placed there. I worked too late to trust him to survive anywhere but in the house. And in the house, there was also a prey animal. Mom's anger became more incessant. Each day she had a new gripe. Too smelly. Too noisy. The cleaning lady was complaining. Too many feathers. And then there were days when she simply ignored me and showed her disdain by banging things. True, he followed me like an obsequious puppy, and was good company, but he was running out of room… and time.

Friday was a late night shift for me. I'd start at 4 P.M. and work at least ten hours. Sometimes I did double shifts of sixteen hours, earning time and a half. With no financial help from home, extra money was in demand with me. I secured Crazy Duck in his box, weighted a barbecue grate across the top and left for work. As I reached the door, I heard him quacking, went back and gave him another peek to make sure he was fine. He looked up at me and it occurred to me that he had transformed from a scruffy little duckling into a magnificent bird that looked no different from other ducks. Then I left, passing by the front kitchen. Mom seemed nonchalant and almost pleasant.

"Working late tonight?" she cooed.

"Probably ten hours. I doubt I'll do a double shift."

"Bring me some of their butter, if you can."

"Sure." I thought appeasement might buy some time for my duck.

Intuition is worth its weight in gold but there are times, even when we suspect something, that circumstances are against us. I had to report for work. The bakery did not look kindly on lost time or even tardiness.

The night droned on. An earlier order was backed up when the ovens broke a drive chain. They were short handed on the night shift and enlisted me until 4 a.m. I slept during my break and lunch, too tired to eat. Work on the ovens was hot, sweaty and laborious. The machine set the pace. My job was to take a five loaf pan from the oven and place it on a rack. We wore no gloves. Instead, they furnished burlap pads with a hole cut in one end. The pads heated up but they wouldn't burn. Unfortunately the speed of the bread coming out often caused my hand to slip outside the burlap, in which case I was grabbing a pan with my bare hand. The Supervisors did not deem a burned hand sufficient grounds to get off the ovens.

Throughout the night, I deliberated on the fate of my little friend. I knew his time at home was limited. He had grown too large and needed more space. And mom was being much too indulgent for my friendship to last. When she adopted that sweet tone in her voice she had something planned. She could not understand why I needed Crazy Duck. Yet, he took the place of the companions I could not befriend because of work and school. He comforted me when I was alone. He was the laughter I missed during the day. He alone showed me any affection, any gratitude.

I decided that on arriving home I'd start calling farms and petting zoos to see if they might be interested. At least, I'd know he was safe. I could even visit him and make certain he was well kept. My uncle had a farm near Basking Ridge. Perhaps Cheech might take him, even temporarily would help. It was a race with time and mom's temperament. I had to act quickly.

The house was dark when I arrived. I saw the upstairs curtain move and I knew mom had seen me come home. At five in the morning that was never a good sign. During a lifetime, one learns that instinct is very often accurate, that sinking leap as the heart flutters and the stomach jumps, is very often based on a truth we know but wish were not so. I rushed down the hallway to the large kitchen. The nest was gone and Crazy Duck was nowhere in sight. I was frantic. I raced to the rear door to search the yard but I knew he would not be there. Mom had struck again. Her manipulation always seemed to triumph. She didn't want an animal in her house and she didn't care who got hurt, as long as she won.

It was too early to wake the house though I was certain she was already awake. I slammed the front door on my way out. She must have heard the tires squealing as I floored the gas pedal and shot off. I drove around, trying to think. What would she do with a duck in that period of time? Who could she give it to? Where could she bring it? No, she wouldn't bring it anywhere. She'd order my father to do the dirty work.

How I hated her at that moment. How I despised her. What kind of woman inflicts pain and brings unhappiness simply to exert her will?

It was three hours later when I returned home. She was sitting in the kitchen, stirring cake mix.

"What did you do with my duck?"

No answer.

"I want to know what you did with my goddamn duck? He's my friend, the only friend I have. What did you dooooo with him?"

"I didn't dooooooooo anything with him." She mocked me, victory gleaning in her eyes.

"Then where the frig is he?"

"Don't talk to me in that tone." Her words cut sharply but her face registered fright. In all my life, I had never bucked her with such vehemence.

"I want to know what you did with my duck."

"Your father brought him to a farmer he knows. He'll be safe there and have a lot of room to live." She kept stirring the pot, avoiding my gaze. My eyes were glazed and fierce.

"Where is the farm?"

"I don't know. It belongs to your father's friend."

"Mom, you're a damn liar. Did you bring him to a butcher or something?"

She remained silent. I wanted her to understand how angry I was. I was making a point. She couldn't manipulate the lives of people simply to have her own way. I slammed a kitchen chair against the table. The blow snapped one of the spindles. Her head snapped up.

"Are you crazy? I'll call the cops."

"Go ahead. Call the cops. I'll give you a reason to call the cops, you old witch. You're full of fear and hate and meanness." With that, I stalked out the door and headed to Joey Head's home.

Joey was just coming out his door when I met him.

"She took Crazy Duck."

"Yer mother?"

"Yeah, the old witch got rid of him. I don't even know where to look. Says my father took him to a farm. Bull. He doesn't know any farmers."

"Maybe the Farmer's Market?" He offered. "There's only one poultry guy around. That's where you bought him."

"Got to go!"

"Hey, want me ta see yer dad at work and ask about the farmer?"

"Do it, pal. I'll meet you back here as soon as I check out the market."

He smiled. "Good luck. I kind of like dat duck. See you later."

I sped to the market. The poultry man was loading crates of chickens onto the platform. When he saw me, he smiled.

"How's the duck?"

"He was all right until last night."

"Oh?" He lifted another crate. The chickens clucked and pecked at each other, scurrying to settle.

"My mother brought him somewhere. Or maybe my father. I thought maybe he might be here. Did anyone sell you a duck yesterday?"

"I just came in today. I was sick yesterday and my partner took over. He's on the road. Won't be back for two days."

I hung my head in self remorse.

He stopped loading and looked at me. "I'm sorry about your duck. Did it mean something to you?"

"He's my pet. Some people have a dog. Some have cats. The only thing I had room for was a duck."

"I got three crates of ducks in the back. If you find him, I'll sell him to you for what I paid. I can't give him away."

I must have brightened because he motioned me toward the rear of his store. "Back there."

"Mister, I understand about paying. Money isn't an issue. Thanks. Thanks a lot."

I went into the rear. The crates were piled head high and there were ten or twelve ducks in each crate. They were all white, fully grown, with wide, black eyes, and yellow bills and feet. Nothing distinguished them and I berated myself for not having paid more attention to Crazy Duck's individual features. I hoped Crazy Duck would make himself known. Surely, he'd recognize me and seek me out. But all the ducks were standing shoulder to shoulder and motionless. The power of faith is strong and hope dies slowly and intolerantly. So, I went to the crates and called:

"Here duck duck duck. Here Crazy Duck." Stupid as it sounds, I gazed into the eyes of each duck. Their eyes were bright with alarm. They milled about as I approached. But they all looked so similar; all I could rely on was some sign from Crazy Duck. The first crate produced no result. With failing hopes, I checked the second even more carefully, periodically glancing back to the first crate in hopes my friend would do something familiar, something to say: "Here I am. Lazarus, risen from the dead."

But the second crate yielded no more hope than the first. Once, just once, I thought I saw in the eyes of a single duck, a glint of recognition, as though he were hiding among his own. And then, I understood. I would not find him, and neither would he make himself known. The sad and frail little duck that I nurtured and nursed to health was among his own kind. It was not my place to interfere with the fate he was born to meet. Nor would he reveal himself. He joined with his peers and blocked any recognition. No matter how cruelly they had treated him as a duckling, he was among his own, and joined with them in the security of their nest.

Somehow he had slipped through my fingers; perhaps, through my own carelessness for trusting a wicked entity, and leaving him unguarded. I searched the crates again. The ducks huddled and scurried around the confines of the crate but where once I had seen a glimmer of familiarity, now all the eyes were the same.

Standing there, I lamented as one mourns the passing of a friend. I thought of the empty hours filled by my little friend. I laughed as I recalled him rolling down the staircase, saturated with rye whiskey. And I remembered how proud I felt when he finally grew strong enough to make the leap onto Joey's bed. I thought of the nights he snuggled next to me and nodded to sleep. I was amid this dream when an arm reached up and touched me on the shoulder. It was Joey Head.

"Yer dad says he had nothing to do wit what happened. He doesn't know what yer mother did with Crazy Duck but he said he's sorry."

"Yeah, he's sorry, Joey. So am I."

"Come on, Russ, let's roll the windows down, go for a long drive and talk. I'll put gas in yer wheels."

"Maybe later, Joey. I got something to do."

"Yeah, maybe it's time ya got out a little more. Come around for some pinochle or Friday poker. Maybe date a girl. Hey, if I can get a girl, you can get one."

"Got something to do Joey. I guess It's long overdue. But you've got something there. Time to get out more."

"I'm sorry 'bout the duck. He was a nice little guy. Maybe ya should buy another duckling. Maybe next year?"

"I don't think so, Joey. It's time maybe to go forward, not back. When I was looking for Crazy Duck, he wouldn't come. He had grown up and he was among his own. Even though they'd ultimately die, he couldn't help being what he was. That's the way I've been for twenty years. I wanted to be independent and free, but I kept clinging to the nest. Anyway, I've got something to do. Will you be around tonight?"

He nodded assent. "You ain't making sense as usual, but it sounds good."

I drove to the nest that had been mine for twenty odd years. The house was empty. I packed what belongings I could and loaded them into my car. Struck with nostalgia for the place of my childhood, I returned to the large kitchen. Mom was absent and Dad was working his second job. It was his way of staying sane. Under the sink lay a single feather. It was white and short, as short as the brief span in which my friend and I had bonded.

"Goodbye, Crazy Duck," I whispered, caressing the unmarked feather. I realized it was foolish to cry over a duck. Men don't cry; or, at least, they're not supposed to weep. But I did. I cried for my friend. I cried for the life I was leaving behind. I cried for the empty nest.

I stepped down the hallway and stopped by the telephone desk. Family pictures decorated the top shelf. Dad, mom and me. I studied them as if I'd never seen them before. Then, lifting the picture of my mother I simply nodded my head and whispered:

"Time to go, mom. Got to learn to fly on my own. I don't have much. All I have it this." And with that, I affixed the feather before the alter of the goddess and bowed goodbye. One leaves an offering to the gods lest he offend them and so I did. It was my way of saying goodbye and my way of leaving an empty nest behind me. I knew that time would heal the hurts of growing up. In time mom and I would come to an understanding just as I had with my little duck. In the end it didn't matter how much hurt I endured in the process of going forward. All that would matter would be that a fluffy, little duck had taught me the value of leaving the nest behind.

Epilogue

So now my little tale is done,
The reader's heart is lost or won.
I take my leave and thus depart,
With happy ghosts locked in my heart.

In 1991, I retired from twenty five years of law practice. As none of my four children followed the law, there was no one to assume my business. The ensuing years would be difficult years of transition for me, relocating from metropolitan New Jersey and a high pressure law practice to rural Kentucky. They would be tortured years of loss of purpose, depression, anger and frustration. Only the resurgence of my interest in writing, my love of animals and my wife's strong determination to prompt my talents (if any) finally brought me to internal peace and a sense of usefulness. I am told I have a natural talent for writing and that I touch people with my stories. I hope that this is true, but this sentiment is not the reason for writing. That reason is to share my love and to publish how animals impact our lives on a daily basis. I wrote I had other reasons for writing. This book is also to ask forgiveness. From Poco my Doberman who was caught up in a marital dispute and died for want of love and attention. It was also written for my little Cocker Spaniel, Blackie, who deserved better than a seventeen year old gave her. From her I learned that the capacity to love is infinite.

What an empty world this would be if no animals existed.

Before I abandoned New Jersey, I visited my grandfather's farmlands where Lucky and I had befriended one another. Lord Stirling Road was no longer a dirt packed route, but chip and seal. The metal bridge that crossed its stream remained and there was still evidence that during heavy rains it flooded the road. Years before the area had been declared a wetland and the State bought the lands and tore down the original buildings. The farmhouse was gone along with all the barns, the caretaker's house, the corn crib, the diary barn even the fencing.

I had not been there since my last days of hunting in 1953. A wooden shack stood at the entrance to the white stone driveway. The door was locked and there was no attendant about the place. There were some displays of early artifacts found around the property that depicted its early American history but nothing about the people who had owned the farm. This was the place of my freedom, the place where the seed of writing took root, lay dormant and suddenly sprang to life. This was the place of the boy and it was the memory of the man who would revisit it and lock it forever in his heart. All its occupants, save one, were dead.

The land was dead. It was overgrown and tick infested. Gone was the red brick building in which my grandfather lived, gone the silos, the corn crib, the barn where Lucky was stalled, the milking barn, the caretaker's house. The spring fed pump that gushed ice cold, delicious water had been plugged and rendered useless, the screened pavilion was absent and the trellis shaded picnic tables where we enjoyed many, many Sunday dinners were no longer there. The brick barbecues had been bulldozed away, the fencing had been torn down, and the twenty-seven dog houses for the hunting dogs had been removed. The path down to the back cow field was a mere trickle through briars and undergrowth.

I started down the path. To my left, the land was overgrown and the field where I first rode Lucky was non-existent. To my right, the land was marshy and flooded where the State had allowed the river to confiscate the earth. Beyond the marsh, though, was the cleared land where Lucky's paddock had been. Except for the high grass it was relatively open. I worked my way through brush and foliage, flicking off the ticks as they dropped onto my clothing. I passed the place where the telephone pole had been. It no longer leaned precariously because it was no longer there. The memory of the caretaker hanging on that pole as an angry bull tried to batter it down was intact.

There was a single spot in that field almost dead center of the land. I walked there and peered at the ground. The fescue grass was level and short cropped as if something had been grazing there. I decided it must be the place where Lucky had been laid to rest. I had brought with me a small wooden cross and a single rose. It was my goodbye to Lucky. Without thinking, I had brought the cross but nothing to tap it into the ground. As I looked around for a rock, I spotted a man rapidly striding toward me. He had the uniform and look of someone in authority and I assumed he was a Park Ranger or a law enforcement agent, though he lacked a year or two short of thirty. He was lean, sinewy and in good physical condition as he maintained his pace across the field, arriving without any sign of exertion. More importantly, he had the look about him of a man ready to arrest me.

"This is State land. It's closed to the public," he declared as he drew near enough for me to hear him. "You can visit the museum at the front but you can't walk around the grounds. It's a waterfowl sanctuary and wetlands."

"It always did flood a lot. My grandfather used to own this land. He died when I was nine." I turned and pointed to the roadway. "The main building was right over there. It was a red brick building and there was a huge tree standing in front of it. In summer we'd hang traps on the branches and catch thousands of Japanese beetles. And over there," I continued, pointing toward the open field, "was the caretaker's house, the diary barn and the corn crib. Over to the left my grandfather had twenty-seven hunting dogs of all breeds. I see the well is still there but it's locked. Right around there," I pointed again, "we had picnic tables under an arbor. My grandfather grew grapes on the arbor and in summer it sheltered us from the sun. They had a screen pavilion right next to the house and a leveled area where they played boccia ball every Sunday."

His face relaxed as I recited the litany of buildings and memories and we chatted cordially for another half hour.

"I had an old circus pony, Lucky. Grandpa bought it for me. That was years ago. Lucky contracted pneumonia so they had to put him to sleep. I just retired from law and I'm leaving for Kentucky. I just wanted to say goodbye and mark his grave with a little cross." The caretaker saw the sadness in my eyes. Perhaps he took pity on me.

"There's nothing like a boy's first pony," he commented and then reverently bowed his head as if paying homage to my dead friend.

"No, I guess not. I'll never forget Lucky. Would it be all right if I just laid the cross down? Here in the center of the field? It wouldn't hurt anything. I was told they buried him in the middle of his paddock. I got sick myself so I never saw Lucky again. My mom made sure of that."

He hesitated and remained silent for a time. Clearly he was not used to people with feelings. His original intent had been to run me off but he was a farm boy and he understood the love of animals.

"Hell," he said, "what harm can it do? I'm not supposed to do this but if you hold on for a few minutes, I'll get you a hammer. Then I'm going to inspect another section of the sanctuary but you've got to be gone when I get back. About twenty minutes."

"Fair enough." I said.

He brought me the hammer and I set the cross right where I believed Lucky rested. When I handed him the hammer and thanked him, he had the same satisfied smile on his face that I did.

"I'll make sure it stays up as long as the weather will allow. It floods here every now and then," he said, "but I'll keep it up as long as I can."

I stretched out my hand and thanked him for his understanding. He wished me luck in Kentucky. We worked our way back across the field. I turned once more to brand the place into my heart. When I did, the sun had broken through the clouds and the cross was glittering like gold. I guessed it was Lucky's way of saying he was pleased I remembered him. There was no way I could write his story without our meeting again somewhere.

I imagine the cross has long disintegrated and fallen but it matters little now because I also erected a monument in my heart and it is in my heart that Lucky will always shine.